TOPICS IN
CHINESE LITERATURE

HARVARD–YENCHING INSTITUTE STUDIES
VOLUME III

TOPICS IN CHINESE LITERATURE

Outlines and Bibliographies

BY

JAMES ROBERT HIGHTOWER

HARVARD UNIVERSITY

HARVARD UNIVERSITY PRESS
CAMBRIDGE, MASSACHUSETTS

DISTRIBUTED IN GREAT BRITAIN BY
OXFORD UNIVERSITY PRESS, LONDON

SBN 674–89520–7

PRINTED IN THE UNITED STATES OF AMERICA

FOREWORD

This is the fifth reprinting of the 1953 edition of *Topics in Chinese Literature*, which differs from the original publication of 1950 only as pointed out in the author's preface to the second edition. Professor Hightower is now preparing a second revision with an expanded bibliography as well as some changes and additions to the text. As it may well be a couple of years before this new edition is available, the work is being reprinted in its present form in order to meet the continuing demand for this basic handbook on Chinese literature.

GLEN W. BAXTER
Associate Director
Harvard-Yenching Institute

16 March 1971

The purpose of these outlines is to provide students with some of the factual data on which an historical survey of Chinese literature may be based. The topics here outlined are for the most part literary styles or genres. The sequence of topics is roughly chronological, and the treatment of each topic attempts to give an historical survey of the subject, including related genres. Technical terms have been used freely and defined on their first occurrence. Titles of books and their authors have been kept to a minimum; not all of the important ones are mentioned; but those which do occur are to be considered significant in their context.

The contents of these outlines is not wholly factual. Controversial points, especially of chronology, could not be avoided, and the very choice of topics to be included involves a strong element of subjective judgment. Because of limitations of space and the intended use of this book I have not entered into a discussion of such points, but in each case have tried to follow the most reliable authority in a given subject. Although specific documentation has been omitted, a list of the most important sources used will be found appended to each chapter under the heading "Authorities." Those to which I am most indebted are marked with an asterisk. Except for the first three chapters these sources consist for the most part of studies in Japanese and Chinese languages; the few existing Western language studies on purely literary topics are seldom of any use. I have relied on these secondary materials for much of the factual matter incorporated in the outlines; however, I am chiefly responsible for arrangement, emphasis, and interpretation. I have been aware of a tendency toward over-simplification, a fault inescapable in any attempt to reduce complex literary phenomena to an intelligible scheme. I hope that my readers will bear in mind that this work is concerned with establishing norms, not in noting exceptions.

Dates have been supplied where possible on the first occurrence of an author's name; these are all from Chiang Liang-fu's *Li-tai ming-jen nien li pei-chuan tsung-piao* or failing that, from T'an cheng-pi's *Chung-kuo wen-hsüeh-chia ta tz'u-tien,* a less reliable source.

The translations listed are intended primarily to provide readers without a knowledge of Chinese with accessible specimens of the genres discussed in the outlines. The entries are selective in that the existence of a good translation of a given piece makes unnecessary the inclusion of an unsatisfactory one. However, preference is given to English language translations, so that a good translation into French or German may be followed by a less adequate one into English; in such cases the best translation is starred. Frequently there exists only a single inadequate translation of an important specimen; such are preceded by the symbol ?.

Characters for Chinese terms and proper names occurring in the text are given in the index.

I wish here to express my thanks to the Trustees of the Rockefeller Foundation for a grant which made possible the compilation of these outlines.

Cambridge, Massachusetts, 1949   J. R. H.

PREFACE TO THE SECOND EDITION

In this revised edition I have made a few changes, correcting the mistakes which have been called to my attention and modifying the treatment of Han dynasty verse forms in Chapter VII. Two new chapters have been added, VIII "Five-word and Seven-word Poetry" and XIII "Schools of Sung Poetry." A list of addenda and corrigenda will be found on page 130. I wish to thank Professor Carrington Goodrich of Columbia University and Dr. Richard Irwin of the University of California Library for their helpful criticism of the first edition of these *Topics*.

September, 1952   J. R. H.

CONTENTS

THE CLASSICS

The Classics *(Ching)* make up the canon of the Confucian school. Like all collections of canonical writings, they are of an extremely heterogeneous nature, produced by no one writer and dating from diverse periods. They derive their canonical sanction from their traditional association with the sage Confucius, the connection in some cases being indirect, as of works attributed to his immediate descendants or disciples. The list of works acknowledged to be part of the Canon was not always the same, being established in its present form only during the twelfth century. However, during the Former Han dynasty, when the Confucian school was achieving its position of orthodoxy, six works were accepted as Classics of the first rank: The *Classic of Divination (I ching)*, the *Classic of Documents (Shu ching)*, the *Classic of Songs (Shih ching)*, the *Spring and Autumn [Annals] (Ch'un-ch'iu)*, the *Classic of Ritual (Li ching)*, and the *Classic of Music (Yüeh ching)*. Of these, the *Classic of Music* was a name only, and the *Classic of Ritual* a generic term for a number of handbooks dealing with ritual subjects, of which the books of rites which we know as *Li chi, I li, Chou li,* and *Ta-Tai li-chi* are later arrangements and interpretations. To these were later added, as less important but still orthodox parts of the Canon, the *Confucian Analects (Lun yü)*, the *Mencius (Meng tzu)*, the *Three Commentaries (Kung-yang chuan, Ku-liang chuan,* and *Tso chuan)* on the *Spring and Autumn Annals,* and the lexical work *Erh ya*. Finally the Sung dynasty Neo-confucians singled out two chapters of the *Collection of Ritual* as especially susceptible to the kind of re-interpretation which they were trying to inflict on the Confucian doctrine, and with the success of the new school these chapters became parts of the canon as the *Great Learning (Ta hsüeh)* and the *Happy Mean (Chung yung)*.

Because the Confucian Classics constituted the basic curriculum of the Chinese system of education and were literally memorized by every educated person through most of China's history from Han times on, they must be considered together as a corpus of works with unsurpassed influence on all of subsequent literature. In addition a few of the Classics possess intrinsic literary merit and are worth studying as literary works independently of their importance as influences. The *Classic of Songs* and the *Tso chuan* are outstanding examples of poetry and narrative prose and would attract attention without their status as Classics. The works comprising the canon have another importance as the earliest surviving specimens of composition in the Chinese language (excluding inscriptions, which seldom run to more than a few lines of connected text). As such they represent the utilitarian uses to which a language must be put before it is shaped into an instrument capable of artistic literary effects.

For these reasons the study of Chinese literature must begin with a group of works which are associated through no similarity of literary form, content or intent, which are only exceptionally of value as literature, and which are accessible in their original language only through an exacting philological study scarcely rewarded by their interest as literature. The Confucian Classics are briefly discussed in turn below. (The *Mencius* is considered in Chapter II with other philosophical writings.)

The *Classic of Divination* was used as a handbook by the official fortune-tellers of the feudal period and was applied to divination by shuffling stalks of the divining plant. Omen formulae from a variety of sources are distributed under sixty-four hexagrams. These hexagrams are made up of the sixty-four possible permutations of divided and unbroken lines, taken six at a time:

$$\equiv\equiv , \equiv\equiv , \equiv\equiv , \equiv\equiv , \equiv\equiv , \equiv\equiv , \text{ etc.}$$

The hexagram relevant to a given question was established by drawing a series of lots, odd numbers representing unbroken lines and even numbers broken lines. The omen formulae, being succinct and gnomic, were subject to interpretation by the diviner.

Much of the book may have been in existence at the time of Confucius, and there is a late tradition that he produced a commentary on it. This commentary, an ethical and cosmological treatise which takes as a point of departure a word or phrase in the divination text proper, probably was gradually added over a period of a couple of centuries after B.C. 300. Once accepted as a part of the Confucian Canon — as it was by Han times — the *Classic of Divination* provided fertile ground for interpretation, and a good part of Chinese metaphysical and cosmological thinking went into ostensible commentaries on a book which remains hardly understood and perhaps not really very intelligible.

The *Classic of Documents* is a collection of speeches and

exhortations, mostly of high moral tone, attributed to the kings and ministers of highest antiquity down through the first 300 years of the Chou dynasty. In the *Analects* Confucius is twice mentioned as quoting or discussing a line from a *Shu,* and tradition assigned to him the role of editor of the collection, by Han times available only in an incomplete form. A Preface, descriptive of the occasions for the various speeches, and associated with the Han version of the book, was attributed to Confucius. In its present form, only half of the *Classic of Documents* is of pre-Han (and probably pre-Confucian) date, the rest being a fourth century forgery.

The *Classic of Songs* is a collection of literary folk songs, occasional pieces, religious odes, and dynastic hymns, some of them dating from early Chou times and the most recent probably being earlier than Confucius. A late tradition ascribes to him the selection and editing also of this collection, which he must have known in some form and which he used in his teaching. It is generally assumed that the collection as it now exists—and has existed essentially without change since the Han, and probably earlier—underwent a thorough revision at some time to reduce the rhymes to those in a standard dialect, probably that of the Chou court. The folk themes represented are sometimes incorporated into a sophisticated court poetry, which probably also borrowed from popular sources many of the tunes to which the words were sung. These tunes were already lost by Han times.

The *Spring and Autumn Annals* is a chronicle of events in the feudal states from B.C. 721 to 481, arranged after the chronology of the State of Lu, of which Confucius was a native. Confucius is quoted by Mencius as saying, "Yes! It is the *Spring and Autumn* which will make men know me, and it is the *Spring and Autumn* which will make men condemn me." It is generally believed that the *Spring and Autumn Annals* is a fairly reliable chronicle, but commentators have had a hard time trying to justify the claim imputed to Confucius that he could attract attention on the basis of such a work. Three ritual commentaries were known in Han times which elaborated a "praise and blame" interpretation of the *Spring and Autumn Annals,* whereby each entry is to be searched for hidden meanings that could be taken as moral judgments on the event chronicled. These commentaries have become part of the Canon.

The *Kung-yang* and *Ku-liang* commentaries (named after their putative authors) are written in the form of catechisms serving to elucidate the esoteric meanings of the *Spring and Autumn Annals.*

Accessory facts and legends are adduced to bolster up an interpretation. The two texts are more often than not in agreement in
principle, less frequently so in detail.

The *Tso chuan* (authorship uncertain) is a much more lengthy
commentary on the same *Spring and Autumn Annals,* but with sufficient additional detail of fact and legend to constitute an
independent account of the period. Whether or not it is a reliable
history of feudal China, it is a valuable collection of anecdote
and legend with great intrinsic and literary interest.

The four collections of ritual were probably all compiled in
their present form during the Han dynasty, the sources used being
of diverse date. The *Li chi (Collected Ritual)* and the *Ta-Tai li-
chi (Collected Ritual of Tai the Elder)* are the more heterogeneous
in content and show fewer effects of a systematizing editorship.
Only the former is a regular part of the Canon, historical accident
being the only apparent reason. The *Collected Ritual* deals in a
haphazard way with ritual observances appropriate on various
occasions: mourning, birth, capping, marriage, state interviews,
banquets, and sacrifices; it treats of music, dress, archery, and
games. Frequently the rules are illustrated by anecdotes in which
Confucius and his disciples are made to figure.

A much more systematic treatise on selected topics of ritual
practice is the *I li (Ceremony and Ritual).* In it are included
the rules of conduct for an individual in several situations, each
dealt with exhaustively and unadorned with historical or legendary
examples.

The *Chou li (Ritual of the Chou Dynasty)* is better described
by its alternative name *Chou kuan (Officials of the Chou).* It is
a highly systematized description of the hundreds of officials who
ideally might have been employed in the feudal courts. Their
functions, rights, obligations and dress are given in varying
degrees of detail. This work is supposed to be older than the
Han, though no one now believes that it describes a government
that actually functioned.

The *Confucian Analects* records the conversations of Confucius
(5th century B.C.) with his disciples; included are a couple of
chapters similar to the documents which went into the *Classic of
Documents* and the *Collected Ritual.* It is probably the most
reliable source for early Confucian doctrine.

Authorities

Henri Maspero, *La Chine antique,* pp. 427-453, 545-552 (1927).

Arthur Waley, "The Book of Changes," *Bulletin of the Museum of Far Eastern Antiquities (BMFEA)* 5(1933).121-142.

Paul Pelliot, "Le *Chou king* en charactères anciens et le *Chang chou che wen,*" *Mémoires concernant l'Asie orientale* 2.123-177 (1916).

H. G. Creel, *Studies in Early Chinese Culture,* pp. 55-95 (1937).

Marcel Granet, *Festivals and Songs of Ancient China,* 239 pp. (1932).

Ch'i Ssu-ho, "Professor William Hung on the Ch'un-ch'iu," *Yenching Journal of Social Studies,* 1(1938).49-71.

P'i Hsi-jui 皮錫瑞, *Ching-hsüeh t'ung-lun* 經學通論, 5 vols. (1907).

Honda Nariyuki 本田成之, *Shina keigaku shiron* 支那經學史論, 411 pp. (1927).

Fan Wen-lan 范文瀾, *Ch'ün-ching kai-lun* 羣經概論, 420 pp. (1933).

Hung Yeh 洪業, *Ch'un-ch'iu ching-chuan yin-te hsü* 春秋經傳引得序, 106 pp. (1937).

Translations

1. *I ching*

   James Legge, *The Yi King,* 444 pp., vol. 16 in *Sacred Books of the East* (1882).
   Richard Wilhelm, *I Ging, das Buch der Wandlungen,* 2 vols. 282, 262 pp. (1924).

2. *Shu ching*

   J. Legge, *The Shoo King,* 735 pp., vol. 3 in *The Chinese Classics* (1865).

3. *Shih ching*

Arthur Waley, *The Book of Songs*, 349 pp. (1937).

B. Karlgren, "The Book of Odes," *BMFEA* 16(1944).171-256, 17(1945).65-100.

4. *Ch'un-ch'iu* and Commentaries

J. Legge, *The Ch'un Ts'ew, with Tso Chuen*, 863 pp., vol. 5 in *The Chinese Classics* (1872). The Prolegomena, pp. 54-81, contains specimen translations of the commentaries of *Kung-yang* and *Ku-liang*.

5. *Li chi*

J. Legge, *Li Ki*, vols. 27-28 in *SBE*, 479, 470 pp. (1885).

S. Couvreur, *Li Ki*, 2 vols. 788, 708 pp. (1899).

6. *I li*

Steele, *The I-Li*, 2 vols., 285, 237 pp. (1917).

S. Couvreur, *Cérémonial*, 667 pp. (1928).

7. *Chou li*

E. Biot, *Le Tcheou-li*, 2 vols., 500, 611 pp. (1851).

8. *Ta-Tai li-chi*

R. Wilhelm, *Li Gi, das Buch der Sitte des älteren und jüngeren Dai*, 449 pp. (1930).

9. *Lun yü*

J. Legge, *Confucian Analects*, 354 pp., vol. 1 in *The Chinese Classics* (1893).

A. Waley, *The Analects of Confucius*, 262 pp. ·(1938).

EARLY EXPOSITORY PROSE: THE PHILOSOPHERS

Like the Confucian Classics, the writings of the early philosophers are important in Chinese literary history for other reasons than their merit as literature. They are among the few surviving texts of feudal and Han China, and as such attract perhaps more attention than they would in a more richly documented period. But aside from the few philosophers whose writings are literature in the narrow meaning of the term, their contribution to the development of prose as an adequate tool for expository writing is of the first importance. In their writings may be seen in rudimentary form the techniques of style and organization, of logic and argumentation that were exploited by later writers for purely literary ends. Even the effective use of written Chinese as a means of communication is probably in some degree due to the carping of the sophists and the verbal gymnastics of the logicians. Dialogue and anecdote first appear in the writings of the philosophers, and the allegorical fantasies of the Taoists are the earliest examples of what may be called imaginative literature. The concern with ethics of most Chinese literary theory is probably a reflection of the dominant topic of the philosophers. Thus literary form, technique, and theory are all in their debt. The following is a brief survey of philosophical writing through the Han dynasty.

The late feudal period in China witnessed a remarkable growth of philosophical schools, many of which left representative written records of doctrine attributed usually to the founder of the school. The earliest in date of these records and the least systematic in form is the *Analects of Confucius (Lun Yü)*, containing the pronouncements of the Master on various subjects as recorded by his immediate disciples. Not much more system is apparent in the *Book of Mencius (Meng tzu)*, a similar record of Mencius' (B.C. 372-289) opinions, put in the form of a series of interviews and conversations. However, *Mencius* is less disjointed; the remarks are placed in a context and are consequently not so ambiguous. It marks a considerable advance in the evolution of a form suitable for the propagation of philosophical doctrine. The *Mencius* is a model of straightforward expository prose. Another Confucian school, slightly later than that of Mencius, is represented by the *Hsün tzu,* a series of disquisitions on controversial topics attributed to *Hsün Ch'ing* (*ca.* B.C. 300), in which the dialog form has given place to the essay. The result is a more impersonal style than that of Mencius.

Slightly earlier than Mencius, Mo Ti (5th c. B.C.) established a school whose only surviving writings are incorporated in the *Mo tzu,* a diffuse and repetitive conglomeration of arguments chiefly directed against the Confucians. The style is verbose and uninspired, though the school of logicians associated with that of Mo Ti made a contribution to the development of prose style by pointing out awkward anomalies in contemporary written Chinese. *Mo tzu* is the earliest surviving text containing an exposition of doctrine by topics.

The Taoist school produced the most interesting texts from a literary point of view. Representing a transcendent mysticism, the Taoists denied the adequacy of written documents to present a truth in its nature inexpressible. Illogically they insisted on writing and, in their efforts to define the indefinable, composed works marked by profound insight and poetic imagination. One characteristic of the writings of the school is the extensive use of anecdote and analogy, as distinct from the appeal to authority by allusion so typical of the Confucians.

The first of their texts, the *Chuang tzu* (4th c. B.C.), is a unique monument of Chinese prose style and occupies a high place among all Chinese prose literature. Because of later additions, it is not a consistent exposition of Taoist doctrine, nor uniformly of high literary quality.

The *Tao te ching* is probably later than the earliest parts of the *Chuang tzu,* and is more likely the work of one author. Most of it is in verse. The doctrine obscurely expressed in its brief compass has come to represent the original philosophic Taoism to Western readers, and it is the book most often translated from the Chinese.

Lieh tzu is a compilation of disputed date. If it is pre-Han, it is probably later than *Chuang tzu,* which it somewhat resembles in tone and form. In style it tends to be rather more simple. Chapter seven is devoted to the doctrines of Yang Chu, an epicurean Taoist.

The *Huai-nan tzu* is a collection of Taoist writings of different dates compiled under the patronage of Liu An, Prince of Huai-nan (B.C. ?-122).

The Legalist school, advocating a ruthless totalitarian state, borrowed their metaphysics from the Taoists and their technique of

argumentation from the Mohists and the Confucians.   Three texts
represent most of the writings of the school.

The *Book of Lord Shang (Shang-chün shu)* is a handbook for
princes, similar to Machiavelli's famous treatise both in form and
in its amoral opportunism.   It pretends to be the work of Wei Yang,
Lord of Shang (d. B.C. 338), the advisor to Duke Hsiao of Ch'in.
His is only a cover-name for a book composed perhaps as much as a
century later.

The *Han fei tzu* probably contains the actual writings of the
historical Han Fei (d. B.C. 233); at least some chapters are
presented as the memorials which he submitted to the King of Ch'in.
His theories and recommendations tend to be grouped in numerical
categories: "Eight Villainies," "Ten Faults," "Three Precautions,"
etc.   Each essay is a well-ordered piece of argumentative prose,
illustrated by anecdote and example, and written in a straightforward and unambiguous style well suited to the matter.

The *Kuan tzu* is a text of uncertain date incorporating a mass
of semi-legendary material about a famous advisor to Duke Huan of
Ch'i, Kuan I-wu, who died in the middle of the seventh century B.C.
It ascribes to him the organization of a legalist government, which
is described in considerable detail.

By Han times the several philosophical schools tended to lose
their doctrinal individuality and merge into a syncretic hodgepodge,
so that it could be said of a given writer only that he tended to
be more sympathetic to one or another of them.   This syncretism is
already apparent in the *Lü-shih ch'un-ch'iu,* a congeries of ritual
tracts prescribing seasonal activities, of legalist and Taoist
theorizing, and containing a number of legends and anecdotes
inserted to illustrate points of doctrine.   Traditionally this work
was compiled under the patronage of Lü Pu-wei (d. B.C. 235), a
rich merchant who had befriended the Ch'in prince whose son became
ruler of all China as Ch'in Shih-huang-ti.   Despite its heterogeneous
content, the *Lü-shih ch'un-ch'iu* is written in a clear and uniform
style.   It shows a high degree of organization in its distribution
of materials under three general headings (Prescriptions, Considerations, Discussions), but no organic unity.

The *Hsin yü* of Lu Chia (d. *ca.* B.C. 180) is an ostensibly
Confucian treatise on government by a famous courtier and advisor
to the first two emperors of the Han dynasty.   Possibly the idea
of this "Mirror for Princes" was borrowed from one of the legalist
works such as the *Shang-chün shu.*   The present text of the *Hsin yü*
has been looked on with suspicion and may not be the original work

of Lu Chia.

The *Hsin shu* is an analogous collection of essays by Chia I (B.C. 201-169). Included is the "Discussion of the Faults of Ch'in," justly famous for its acute reasoning and brilliance of style.

Tung Chung-shu (d. *ca.* B.C. 140) developed a theory of government on the basis of the *Spring and Autumn Annals* that played a considerable part in the formation of orthodox Confucianism in Han times. Like his contemporaries, he was favorably disposed toward ideas properly a part of non-Confucian systems and incorporated *yin-yang* metaphysics and omen lore into his *Ch'un-ch'iu fan-lu.*

Yang Hsiung (B.C. 53- A.D. 18), much admired in Han times as a poet and philosopher, wrote two books based on canonical works: the *Fa yen* in imitation of the *Confucian Analects,* and the *T'ai hsüan ching* modeled on the *Classic of Divination.* The former is sententious and aphoristic, the latter as murky and impenetrable as its prototype.

The *Discourses on Salt and Iron (Yen t'ieh lun)* of Huan K'uan (*fl.* B.C. 75) is as much a philosophical work as many others so classified in Chinese bibliographies. However, it is more limited in scope, dealing specifically with a problem of government, and cast in the form of a debate between the supporters of government monopoly of those commodities and their opponents. The debate actually occurred (*ca.* B.C. 83), but the *Discourses* is no more a stenographic account of the debate than are the speeches in *Mencius* a record of actual conversations.

The lengthy and heterogeneous *Disquisitions (Lun heng)* of Wang Ch'ung (A.D. 27-after 100) contains a most original and penetrating criticism of superstition and fallacy which does not even spare the sacrosanct Classics. The edge of Wang Ch'ung's censure is frequently blunted by his excessively literal mind on which metaphor and hyperbole are alike wasted. This, his only surviving work, is of especial interest for the inclusion of several paragraphs of literary theory and criticism.

Wang Fu (2nd c. A.D.) wrote a criticism of government and morals, the *Ch'ien-fu lun,* in a series of short essays. In form the *Ch'ien-fu lun* belongs with the *Hsin yü,* while his subject matter is more comparable with the *Lun heng;* however, he shows less originality than either Lu Chia or Wang Ch'ung.

The *Shen chien* of Hsün Yüeh (148-209) is a guide for princes similar to the *Ch'ien-fu lun.* Hsün Yüeh is better known as a historian.

A short work, *The Study of Human Abilities (Jen wu chih)* by Liu Shao (d. middle of 3rd c.) continues the tradition of Confucian rationalism into a time when it was becoming an anachronism. This book is a highly systematized treatise on the capacities and dispositions of men reminiscent sometimes of the Theophrastan character writers. The style tends already to use the sort of parallel constructions which typify the prose of the Six Dynasties.

Authorities

A. Forke, *Geschichte der alten chinesischen Philosophie*, 592 pp. (1927).

———, *Geschichte der mittelalterlichen chinesischen Philosophie*, pp. 1-175 (1934).

Fung Yu-lan, *A History of Chinese Philosophy: The Period of the Philosophers*, 455 pp. (1937).

*A. Waley, *Three Ways of Thought in Ancient China*, 275 pp. (1939).

Hu Shih, *The Development of the Logical Method in China*, pp. 53-118 (1922).

H. Maspero, "Notes sur la logique de Mo-tseu et de son école," *T'oung Pao* (1927).1-64.

O. Franke, *Studien zur Geschichte des Konfuzianischen Dogmas und der chinesischen Staatsreligion. Das Problem des Tsch'un-ts'iu und Tung Tschung-schu's tsch'un-ts'iu fan-lu*, 329 pp. (1920).

Woo Kang, *Les trois théories politiques du Tch'ouen ts'ieou, interprétées par Tong Tchong-chou d'après les principes de l'école de Kong-yang*, 254 pp. (1932).

Translations

1. *The Confucian School*

> J. Legge, *The Works of Mencius*, 587 pp., vol. 2 in *The Chinese Classics* (1895²).
> H. Dubs, *The Works of Hsün tzu*, 336 pp. (1928).

2. *The Mohists*

> A. Forke, *Mê Ti*, 638 pp. (1922).
> Y. P. Mei, *The Ethical and Political Works of Motse*, 275 pp. (Selections) (1930).

3. *The Taoists*

> H. Giles, *Chuang Tzu*, 454 pp. (1889).
> Fung Yu-lan, *Chuang tzu*, 157 pp. (1931) (Chapters 1-7 of *Chuang tzu*).

A. Waley, *The Way and its Power*, 257 pp. (1935).

R. Wilhelm, *Liä Dsi, das wahre Buch vom quellenden Urgrund*, 175 pp. (1923).

L. Wieger, *Lie tzeu*, pp. 66-199 in *Les Pères du système taoiste* (1913).

L. Giles, *Taoist Teachings from the Book of Lieh Tzu*, 121 pp. (Selections) (1912).

A. Forke, *Yang Chu's Garden of Pleasure*, 64 pp. (Chapter 7 of *Lieh tzu*) (1912).

E. Morgan, *Tao the Great Luminant, essays from Huai-nan tzu*, 287 pp. (Selections) (1935).

4. *The Legalists*

W. K. Liao, *The Complete Works of Han fei tzu*, vol. 1, 310 pp. (1939).

J. J. L. Duyvendak, *The Book of Lord Shang*, 346 pp. (1928).

5. *Syncretic Works*

R. Wilhelm, *Frühling und Herbst des Lü Bu We*, 542 pp. (1928).

A. von Gabain, "Ein Fürstenspiegel: Das *Sin-yü* des Lu Kia," *Mitteilungen des Seminars für Orientalischen Sprachen (MSOS)* 33(1930).1-82.

E. M. Gale, *Discourses on Salt and Iron*, Chapters I-XIX, 165 pp. (1931).Chapters XX-XXVIII, *Journal of the North China Branch of the Royal Asiatic Society (JNCBRAS)* 65(1934). 73-110.

E. von Zach, *Fa yen: Wörter strenger Ermahnung*, (?1940).

A. Forke, *Lun Heng*, vol. 1, 557 pp. (1907); vol. 2, 536 pp. (1911).

J. K. Shryock, *The Study of Human Abilities, The Jen wu chih of Li Shao*, 168 pp. (1937).

III

EARLY NARRATIVE PROSE: HISTORY, FICTION, AND ANECDOTE

Many of the chapters of the *Classic of Documents* are neither a record of fact nor a faithful transcript of legend, but represent a rationalization of legend into pseudo-history. Belonging to this genre of euhemerized history are the *I Chou-shu* and the *Shang-shu ta-chuan,* dealing with the legends centered about the founding of the Chou dynasty. The former is a heavy, unimaginative work written in a style similar to that of the *Classic of Documents;* the latter, known today from collected fragments, probably belongs to the second century B.C. Neither is of much interest as literature.

It was the converse process of elaborating history into fiction that produced some of the best writing in pre-Han China and brought the art of narration up to the level of the expository technique practiced by the most skillful of the philosophical essayists. The form of this fictionalized history is consistently biographical or anecdotal; the subjects are in the first place famous rulers and secondly men of note associated with them. The biographies of the former are necessarily bound up with the fortunes of the states they ruled; the latter are sometimes shown serving a succession of masters, especially when the hero is one of the peripatetic philosophers. Each of the five hegemons became the subject for a fictional biography; the best known are the stories of Duke Wen of Chin (in *Tso chuan* and *Kuo yü*) and King Kou-chien of Yüeh (*Kuo yü, Shih chi,* and *Wu-Yüeh ch'un-ch'iu*). Nearly every general, statesman, and philosopher whose name has come down to us seems to have figured as a character in a story; some such heroes, like Su Ch'in, are probably completely fictitious. There are two methods of dealing with the hero: one is a consecutive account of a man's life, for example the biography of the famous general Wu Ch'i or the statesman Fan Li; the other is a disconnected collection of anecdotes about a figure, designed to illustrate his most prominent traits of character or, in the case of a philosopher, to demonstrate his teachings. The connection of this last genre with the "philosophical" writings is obvious, and there are doubtful works like the *Kuan tzu* that could be classified under either head. The predominantly fictional motive of the *K'ung-tzu chia-yü,* a series of anecdotes about Confucius brought together by Wang Su (195-256) from earlier sources, and a similar work devoted to Yen Ying (6th c. B.C.), the *Yen-tzu ch'un-ch'iu,* is sufficiently apparent, however, and they belong with the other works written as narrative.

These originally independent stories were combined, perhaps even before Han times, into professedly historical works, and it is in this garb that they have survived. It is not certain whether the compilers of the *Tso chuan,* the *Kuo yü,* and the *Chan-kuo ts'e* thought they were writing history; there is a historical basis for the events which they chronicle, but the elaboration of those events, the long conversations, sophistical or moralizing, are either derived from pre-existing fictional accounts or made up for the occasion. These composite works mark a step toward the development of a more complex kind of historical narrative and give promise of a genuine syncretic history which might deal with the complexity of real events more adequately than the simple chronicles kept by official recorders.

The *Tso chuan,* traditionally by a contempory of Confucius, but compiled possibly as late as the second century B.C., in its present form serves as a commentary on the *Spring and Autumn Annals.* It provides a detailed background for the events therein chronicled and in addition contains brief paragraphs of exegesis on the entries in the *Annals* treated as Confucius' handbook for moral instruction in the same manner as the *Kung-yang* and *Ku-liang* commentaries. Because of the nature of the *Annals* with which it is associated, the *Tso chuan* has no unity in its treatment of events; widely separated paragraphs deal with the same subject, and the history of the feudal states is not recounted from the point of view of any one of them in a way that might give the record some coherence. It has been asserted that the *Tso chuan* was not at first connected with the *Annals,* and that the original work was cut up and its parts distributed under the entries in the *Annals* to make the commentary. At any rate, for whatever purpose it was compiled, the *Tso chuan* is based on a pre-existing body of historical fiction, of which it may be taken, for literary purposes, as the finest anthology. Its narrative style is straightforward and unadorned; it achieves its most dramatic effects with an economy and precision that are unique in the whole range of Chinese literature.

Dealing with the same events covered by the *Tso chuan* and in fact sharing with it whole paragraphs almost identical in phrasing, is the *Conversations from the States (Kuo yü),* which has tradi-

15

tionally been ascribed to the putative author of the *Tso chuan*.
The similarities (as well as the differences) between the two are
probably best explained as resulting from the use in each of
similar or identical fictional narratives which existed independently of these compilations. The *Conversations* divides its
material up among eight feudal states; however, it does not
attempt a consecutive account of events in those states, but
gives a series of anecdotes, each being the point of departure for
a speech or series of speeches. Some are the usual moralizing of
ministers of state, some the more effective pleas of concubines to
their masters. Diviners and soothsayers figure prominently and
make frequent predictions—always verified—of the outcome of a
given situation. The *Conversations* relies on dialog for its
interest, and shows a more rudimentary narrative technique than
the *Tso chuan*.

Even as examples of imaginary oratory the *Conversations* is
inferior to the *Intrigues of the Warring States (Chan-kuo ts'e)*,
a vivid fictional presentation of the part played by itinerant
politicians in late feudal times, peddling their schemes, making
and breaking leagues and alliances between the feudal courts, in
everything relying on the sophistical cleverness of their tongues.
Both the date and the authorship of the *Intrigues* are uncertain,
but it was probably compiled during the second century B.C. Like
the *Conversations,* the *Intrigues* is divided into sections devoted
to each of twelve states, the materials under each being in rough
chronological order from B.C. 475 to B.C. 220. If anything, the
historical basis for the *Intrigues* is even slighter than that of
the *Tso chuan* and the *Conversations,* some of the chief characters
being wholly imaginary. If the rhetoric of the longer speeches is
sometimes artificial and boring, the interest of the book is
maintained by an inexhaustible supply of anecdote and contrived
situations of great complexity. The *Intrigues* is unique among
these works for having recognizably humorous passages.

Early in Han times Lu Chia wrote an account of the struggle
for power between Hsiang Yü and Liu Pang following the collapse of
the Ch'in dynasty. This work, the *Ch'u-Han ch'un-ch'iu,* has been
lost as an independent book; however, Ssu-ma Ch'ien says that he
used it in his *Historical Records,* and it is probable that the
Ch'u-Han ch'un-ch'iu is incorporated in that book as the "Annals"
of Hsiang Yü and of Han Kao-tsu (Liu Pang). If the account in
Ssu-ma Ch'ien is actually due to Lu Chia, he must take a high rank
among Chinese writers of narrative. The historicity of the

conflict is beyond question, but the details of the battles and the speeches must be the invention of the narrator. The death scene of Hsiang Yü is a most impressive climax to the dramatic struggle between well-matched protagonists.

Two works of Later Han date attempt to give a similar account of the long struggle between the states of Wu and Yüeh in the fifth century B.C. The *Wu-Yüeh ch'un-ch'iu* by Chao Yeh (*fl.* 40) includes the stories of Kings Ho-lü and Fu-ch'ai of Wu and Kou-chien of Yüeh; in addition the famous ministers of those rulers, Wu Tzu-hsü and Fan Li, are treated at length. It is likely that the *Wu-Yüeh ch'un-ch'iu* has put together pre-existing fictional biographies of those persons. The *Yüeh chüeh shu* by Yüan K'ang (*fl.* 40) deals also with the same two states, but includes a geographical description of their territories as well as historical and apocryphal stories about their rulers. Stylistically it is considered superior to the *Wu-Yüeh ch'un-ch'iu*.

It is only a step from fiction treated as history to genuine history with an admixture of fiction. The first great history of China, the *Historical Records (Shih chi)*, was written by Ssu-ma Ch'ien (B.C. 145-?90). Although he made free use of fictional sources, he seems to have made some attempt to relegate the less historical accounts to a separate section of his book, the *lieh chuan*, while the obviously legendary has been eliminated altogether. He incorporates much of the *Classic of Documents*, the *Tso chuan*, and the *Intrigues of the States* with only minor changes. Many of his sources, such as the *Ch'u-Han ch'un-ch'iu*, have been since lost. The *Historical Records* is essentially a compilation of pre-existing materials arranged to make a history of China from the earliest (legendary) period to Ssu-ma Ch'ien's own times. The book is divided into five sections: (1) twelve Annals of the Rulers (*pen chi*), tracing the sequence of political events as they affected the ruling houses; (2) ten Chronological Tables (*piao*), giving genealogies in tabular form of ruling houses and the feudal courts; (3) eight Essays *(shu)* on subjects considered basic to the functioning of the state: rites, music, musical tubes, calendar, astronomy, the *feng* and *shan* sacrifices, waterways, and trade; (4) thirty "Hereditary Families" (*shih chia*), summary accounts of the more important feudal states, and including biographies of a few outstanding individuals, such as Confucius, who did not have the status of feudal lord; (5) seventy Monographs (*lieh chuan*) consisting for the most part of biographies of pairs of individuals whose lives seemed to follow a common pattern. In this section

17

are included some miscellaneous essays on foreign states, on divination and fortune-telling, and finally Ssu-ma Ch'ien's own autobiography, in so far as it relates to his reasons for compiling his history.

The *History of the Former Han Dynasty (Han shu)* by the Pan family (especially Pan Ku, A.D. 32-92) is the first of the so-called Dynastic Histories, and is devoted to the period from the founding of the Han to the interregnum of Wang Mang (8-23 A.D.). The method by which it was compiled was borrowed from Ssu-ma Ch'ien, likewise the main divisions under which the materials are arranged. However, some changes were introduced. The virtual disappearance of feudalism in Han times caused the omission in the *Han shu* of the section on Hereditary Families. Essays were supplied for three new topics: natural phenomena *(wu hsing)*, geography *(ti-li)*, and bibliography (*i-wen*). The last is of great importance in providing a list of books in the Imperial Archives at the beginning of the first century. From it we can get an idea of the extent of ancient Chinese literature, much of which has since been lost. Because he was dealing with a more fully documented period than Ssu-ma Ch'ien, Pan Ku's history is on the whole a more reliable record of events; at the same time it is more pedestrian and from a literary point of view less interesting. Still, Pan Ku, like Ssu-ma Ch'ien, was a writer of note, aside from his work as a historian.

The *History of the Former Han Dynasty* in turn served as the basis for a condensation by Hsün Yüeh (author of the *Shen chien*) entitled *Records of the Han (Han chi)*, which contains a few original contributions (chiefly moral essays) by its author. The *Records of the Han* essentially follows the Annals section of the *Han shu,* but materials there relegated to the Essays and Monographs have been drawn upon to fill out the sequence of events. Dealing primarily with political history, the *Records of the Han* is little contaminated by fictional elements.

In the Han period several collections were made of anecdotes, traditional and contemporary. The first of these, the *Han-shih wai-chuan* by Han Ying (*fl.* B.C. 157), is an ostensible commentary on the *Classic of Songs* containing a heterogeneous sampling of anecdotes from the philosophers along with moral disquisitions from the same source, each ending with a quotation of a line from the *Classic of Songs.* The immediate model was *Hsün tzu,* but the book itself is not philosophical.

Liu Hsiang (77-6 B.C.) further developed the form in his

Shuo yüan, similar in content, but put together around topical headings, and the *Hsin hsü,* perhaps a supplement to the *Shuo yüan.* His *Stories of Famous Women (Lieh nü chuan)* is a more specialized collection of moral anecdotes about women in history and legend. Again the stories are arranged as illustrations of specific virtues or faults.

One early (pre-Han) fictional travelogue has survived, the *Travels of the Emperor Mu,* a dry chronicle of an imaginary trip to the far west.

Authorities

Henri Maspero, *La Chine antique*, pp. 581-596.

——————, "Le roman de Sou Ts'in," *Études Asiatiques* 2(1925).
127-141.

——————, "Legendes mythologiques dans le *Chou King*," *Journal Asiatique (JA)* 204(1925).1-100.

Translations

1. *Euhemerized History*

    J. Legge, *The Shoo King*, vol. 3 in *The Chinese Classics.*

2. *Fictional Biography*

    E. Chavannes, *Les Mémoires historiques de Se-ma Ts'ien,* vols. 4 and 5 *(Shih chi).*

    A. Forke, "Yen Ying, Staatsmann und Philosoph, und das *Yen-tse tch'un-tch'iu,*" *Hirth Anniversary Volume*, pp. 101-144, esp. pp. 107-125.

    George Kao, *Chinese Wit and Humor*, pp. 37-46 *(Yen-tzu ch'un ch'iu).*

    Cheng Lin, *Prince Dan of Yann*, 13 pp. (1946).

    D. Bodde, *Statesman, Patriot and General in Ancient China,* 75 pp. (1940).

3. *Fiction as History*

    J. Legge, *The Ch'un Ts'ew with the Tso Chuen.*

    S. Couvreur, *Tch'ouen Ts'iou et Tso Tchouan*, 3 vols. (1914).

    C. de Harlez, "Koue yü (Discours des Royaumes)" 1re partie. *JA* 9.2(1893).373-419, 3(1894).5-91; 2e partie, Louvain, 1895.

    George Kao, *Chinese Wit and Humor*, pp. 47-57 (translations from *Chan-kuo ts'e).*

    E. Chavannes, *Les Mémoires historiques de Se-ma Ts'ien,* 2.247-405 *(Ch'u-Han ch'un-ch'iu).*

4. *History with Fictional Admixture*

    E. Chavannes, *Les Mémoires historiques de Se-ma Ts'ien,* vols. 1-3.

    H. H. Dubs, *History of the Former Han Dynasty* by Pan Ku, 2 vols. (1938, 1940).

F. Hirth, "The Story of Chang K'ien," *JAOS* 37(1917).89-152.

5. *Collections of Anecdotes*

S. F. Balfour, "Fragments from *Gallery of Chinese Women* or *Lieh nü chuan*," *Tien Hsia Monthly* 10.3(March 1940).265-283.

L. Wieger, *A History of Religious Beliefs and Philosophical Opinions in China*, pp. 312-14 (specimens from *Hsin-hsü* and *Shuo yüan*).

6. *Imaginary Travels*

Cheng Te-k'un, "The Travels of the Emperor Mu," *JNCBRAS* 64 (1933).124-142; 65(1934).128-149.

IV

CH'U TZ'U AND FU

The poetry anthology known as *Ch'u tz'u* was compiled in its present form and annotated by Wang I (d. A.D. 158), who states that the collection was first put together by Liu Hsiang (B.C. 77-6). There is no mention of a *Ch'u tz'u* by Liu Hsiang in any of the sources before Wang I, and present editions contain a poem by Wang I himself; hence it is uncertain what part Liu Hsiang may have played in selecting and editing the *Ch'u tz'u*. Attributions of authorship of individual poems may all be based on Wang I's judgment, and so have little certainty.

The seventeen titles contained in the anthology may be divided into two groups: poems attributed to Ch'ü Yüan, and imitations of those poems by later writers. The dating and authorship of some poems in both groups are doubtful.

The identity of Ch'ü Yüan himself is so involved with legend that it is probably futile to attempt to separate the poet Ch'ü Yüan, author of the "Li sao," from the loyal minister of King Huai of Ch'u (B.C. 329-299), slandered by envious rivals and misunderstood by his prince, who traditionally gave vent to his just resentment in a series of allegorical poems, and finally drowned himself in despair. The legend of Ch'ü Yüan was crystallized in literary form by Ssu-ma Ch'ien in the "Biography" devoted to him in the *Historical Records,* but parts of that legend are stated or implied in all of the imitations of the "Li sao" collected in the *Ch'u tz'u.*

The *Ch'u tz'u* anthology is best interpreted as a collection of poems in a new form (the *sao*) written on themes stated or traditionally believed to be present in the "Li sao," the prototype of the form, plus a few miscellaneous pieces included as being works of Ch'ü Yüan.

The "Li sao" is a long (374 lines), confused, allegorical poem written in the first person, describing the efforts of its author to find a place for himself in a world where refinement and integrity are not appreciated. His search takes him on an imaginary journey to the farthest reaches of the earth and beyond; he travels up to Heaven and back through time. Sometimes he is seeking a woman at once beautiful and honest; again it is exotic plants and rare fragrances. The symbolism of the poem is as erratic and uncertain as its allegorical themes, but its general import is clear: nowhere does the poet find the understanding and appreciation he feels to be his due.

The "Li sao" is without precedent in Chinese literature. It represents an innovation in theme, form, and metric. The *Classic of Songs* contained allegorical poems, but nothing on such a scale, and nothing so insistently personal. There are variations in the *Classic of Songs* on the basic four-word line, but the "Li sao" uses an entirely different meter, predominantly of six words, with considerable freedom of variation. The rhymes of the "Li sao" are regularly at the end of alternate lines; phonetically they are in close agreement with the rhymes of the *Classic of Songs*.

The text of the "Li sao" is almost certainly corrupt. It has suffered omissions and transpositions that greatly complicate an understanding of its purpose and effectively prevent a systematic interpretation of the allegory, to which Wang I's commentary is not a reliable guide. The many imitations of the "Li sao" contained in the *Ch'u tz'u* help establish themes traditionally believed to be present; all of them reflect the Ch'ü Yüan legend much more strongly than does the "Li sao" itself. There is no point in questioning Ch'ü Yüan's authorship of the "Li sao," but there is room for a fresh interpretation of the poem, independent of the commentaries.

The attribution of the "Nine Hymns" (Chiu ko; actually there are eleven of them) to the author of the "Li sao" accounts for their inclusion in the *Ch'u tz'u*, but it is most unlikely that they are the work of Ch'ü Yüan; a late tradition claims that they were rewritten by him. The first nine appear to be the chants of priests or priestesses of a shamanistic cult who incite a god or tutelary spirit to take physical possession of themselves. The hymns are descriptive incantations perhaps intended to attract the god by a species of word magic. Their sexual character is obscured by the commentators, who insist on treating them as personal and allegorical appeals by Ch'ü Yüan to his ruler. The tenth hymn is a moving lament for soldiers who have died for their country, and the eleventh, of five lines only, appears to be a fragment of a funeral dirge. All of the "Nine Hymns" are written in irregular five- or six-word lines with a caesura indicated by the particle *hsi,* thus differing from the line typical of the "Li sao" and its imitations, where the *hsi* normally occurs at the end of lines which do not rhyme. The date of the "Nine Hymns" is disputed, but they are probably as late as the second century B.C., and belong properly with the Ch'u Song and the *Yüeh-fu*

Hymns of the Han dynasty (Chapter VII).

The "Heavenly Questionings" (T'ien wen), according to Wang I, are a series of questions on mythological subjects written by Ch'ü Yüan to serve as inscriptions on wall paintings in a temple which he visited during his banishment to the south of Ch'u. Whether the figures asked about were actually depicted pictorially is not certain, nor is Ch'ü Yüan's authorship of the "Heavenly Questionings" uncontested. The prosody of the work is nearer to the four-word measure of the *Classic of Songs* than the *sao* form, and the questions are of little literary interest.

The "Nine Declarations" (Chiu chang) are also attributed by Wang I to Ch'ü Yüan. They are similar in meter to the "Li sao," and appear to be short complaints on themes derived from that poem. Frequent use of identical phrases and lines, sometimes in a way that makes a gloss on their occurrence there, is an indication that the "Nine Declarations" are later imitations made when the Ch'ü Yüan legend was well established.

The "Distant Wandering" (Yüan yu), also ascribed to Ch'ü Yüan, is an imitation of the part of the "Li sao" describing Ch'ü Yüan's imaginary travels; here, however, the theme of immortality achieved by the Taoist adept is stated clearly and unambiguously. The ubiquitous "I" of the "Li sao" occurs rarely, but borrowings and references to the "Li sao" make it apparent that the "Distant Wandering" is intended as a re-interpretation of Ch'ü Yüan's voyage. The poet describes the disciplines of breath-control and concentration prerequisite to the physical change making possible untrammeled flight through space. The trip itself is uncomplicated by a search, no allegory clouds the exuberance of this spiritual pilgrimage. In sharp contrast to the mood of disappointment and despair with which the "Li sao" closes, the "Distant Wandering" ends with the achievement by the poet of a mystical union with the Ultimate Beginning. The poem, though derived from the "Li sao," is superior to it in unity and coherence. There is little likelihood that the two are by the same hand.

Two short pieces, mostly in prose, complete the list of works assigned to Ch'ü Yüan. One of them, "The Fisherman" (Yü fu), is incorporated by Ssu-ma Ch'ien in Ch'ü Yüan's biography as describing an encounter between him and a fisherman who offers some practical advice. The other, "Determining a calling by Oracle" (Pu chü), is a series of questions about a suitable course of action presented to a famous diviner, who admits he is unable to answer them. Though part of the Ch'ü Yüan legend, neither is plausible as a composition by Ch'ü Yüan.

Another name appears as the author of the "Nine Persuasions" (Chiu pien), that of Sung Yü. He is an even more shadowy figure than Ch'ü Yüan himself, being mentioned in the *Historical Records* only as a follower of his. A couple of anecdotes in which he figures do nothing to make him more real. For convenience he may be dated around the middle of the third century B.C.; it is also convenient to take him as the author of the works ascribed to him in the *Ch'u tz'u* and elsewhere; at least there is no serious contradiction involved in his case, though it means promoting a very uncertain name to a position of great importance in early Chinese literary history. The "Nine Persuasions" is a series of elegiac laments over the fate of Ch'ü Yüan, put into his mouth, by a convention common to the poems in the *Ch'u tz'u*. They introduce a new lyrical note in Chinese poetry, and show a strong feeling for atmosphere. The meter is irregular and departs from the pattern set by the "Li sao"; the line varies around a 2:4 beat, interrupted by a caesura.

Two variations on a theme, the calling back of the departed soul of Ch'ü Yüan, reflect a religious practice common in early China. The "Summons to the Soul" (Chao hun) is attributed to Sung Yü. It is introduced by a dialog between God and the diviner Yang, who is directed to call back the soul of Ch'ü Yüan that he may live out his term. The diviner calls to the soul, warning of the dangers to be encountered in all four regions of the world, in Heaven and in Hades. This is followed by a description of the delights awaiting the soul if it will return. The "Great Summons" (Ta chao) is an analogous composition variously attributed to Ch'ü Yüan himself and to one of his followers. The relation between the two poems is not clear, but they are certainly connected. Prosodic differences make it unlikely that they are by the same hand. The lush descriptive passages, filled with marvelous rarities and exotic products, are strongly reminiscent of the *fu* proper, and these may well represent an important source of the *fu* style, but the uncertainty of their date and authorship makes the question a difficult one to decide.

The remaining titles in the *Ch'u tz'u* are all attributed to Han writers, from Chia I to Wang I, and here the attributions have every chance of being reliable. These poems are all variations on the same themes and are built around the figure of Ch'ü Yüan. None shows any great originality either of form or treatment.

The *Ch'u tz'u*, then, is an anthology of poems written by or about Ch'ü Yüan, usually in the same metrical form, the *sao*. It is characterized by rhymed lines of irregular length and variable caesura, but not departing far from a six-beat rhythm. The title probably means "Ch'u [state] compositions," and refers to the feudal state of which Ch'ü Yüan and Sung Yü were natives and in which the *sao* form developed.

The poetic genre known as *fu* may be regarded as a development from the *sao,* with which it has in common several characteristics: the long (six- or seven-word) line, the use of caesura, rhyme, and balanced parallel phrases. It differs from the *sao* in being used for a wider range of subjects, with a tendency toward description and exposition rather than subjective lyricism. The prosody of the *fu* is even more free, notably in the *fu* of the Han period, than that of the *sao.* The rhyme pattern is not limited to couplets, and relatively few "empty" words—connectives and prepositions—or pronouns occur in the *fu.* The generally impersonal tone of the *fu* is probably due to its subject matter. Typically the *fu* begins with an introduction in prose, frequently in the form of a dialog, which states the subject to be treated and the events which led to its composition. The *fu* varies in length from a few lines to several hundreds of lines, the more famous pieces tending to be long ones. The descriptive *fu* gets its effects from a piling up of words; descriptive synonyms in a single *fu* tend to exhaust the resources of the dictionary. Several of the Han dynasty writers of *fu* were also lexicographers, and this aspect of the *fu* may come from a precedent established by them; however, verbal virtuosity characterized several of the *sao* poems. The uncertainty of the dates of the latter makes impossible a definite statement of their influence on the *fu;* otherwise the "Summons to the Soul" could be taken as the excuse for the preoccupation of the *fu* with exotic and outlandish products, while the typical *fu* which seeks to persuade (the "Tzu-hsü" and its imitations, the series of *fu* arguing the merits of rival capitals) could be derived ultimately from the incantations of the "Nine Hymns," with some contribution from the "persuasions" practiced by the peripatetic schemers of the *Intrigues of the Warring States.*

The term *fu* was in use before the evolution of the genre for which it came to be the designation. Hence it is not certain that all of the 1004 *fu* by 78 authors listed in the *Han shu* "Essay on Bibliography" were *fu* in the technical sense. No more than 75 of the early *fu* survive, and only a fraction of them are of unquestioned authenticity. Ch'ü Yüan's works are listed as *fu,* also the riddles in rhyme of Hsün-tzu. The earliest author to whom extant *fu* proper are attributed is Sung Yü; all of them are at least suspect, but it is convenient to have a name to attach them to. Among the *fu* assigned to Sung Yü are specimens of most of the types of *fu* that were written in Han times, many of them of the finest quality. They show none of the formalism which later robbed the *fu* of its content and turned it into a poetry of pure form. In the "Master Teng-t'u" Sung Yü uses the *fu* as a vehicle for sophistical argument, conviction being carried more by sensuous description than by logic. In his "Big words" (Ta yen) and "Little words" (Hsiao yen) is the wild hyperbole characteristic of many later *fu*, and not without precedent in the Ch'ü Yüan poems. The most elaborate and highly developed of Sung Yü's *fu* is the "Kao-t'ang," an exuberant exercise in word-magic describing the wonders of Mt. Kao-t'ang. There is less of the lexically bizarre than turns up in most Han *fu*, but the effect is as unearthly as anything in the "Li sao." In yet another vein is the treatment of "The Flute," almost certainly not the work of Sung Yü, but possibly the prototype of the many *fu* eulogizing a musical instrument. The unabashed sensuality of "The Goddess" (Shen-nü fu) found few imitators, but shows the possibilities of the form applied to such a topic.

After Sung Yü the first name represented by a surviving *fu* is Chia I (B.C. 201-169), whose "Owl" is actually the earliest *fu* whose authorship is certain. That the "Owl" is in many ways atypical of Han *fu* generally makes it at least questionable whether the *fu* attributed to Sung Yü are earlier; possibly they were not known to Chia I.

The fully developed *fu* appears around the middle of the second century B.C. with the "Seven Stimuli" (Ch'i fa) of Mei Sheng (B.C. 140) and Ssu-ma Hsiang-ju's (B.C. 179-117) descriptions of hunting parks, the "Tzu-hsü" and "Shang-lin." The poem of Mei Sheng is a rather specialized type of *fu*, clearly related to the "Great Summons" and the "Summons to the Soul," but exhibiting all the qualities of the *fu* proper. The *fu* of Ssu-ma Hsiang-ju are among the best known and most widely read of all the Han *fu*, and served as the models for many imitations, the earliest being the "Yü-lieh" of his follower and admirer, Yang Hsiung (B.C. 53-18 A.D.).

The first of the descriptions of national capitals is the "Two Capitals" of Pan Ku (32-92), a rather mechanical work obviously derived from Ssu-ma Hsiang-ju, but itself the source for imitations, notably by Chang Heng (78-139) and Tso Ssu (*ca.* 300).

Tso Ssu contributed to the development of the theory of the *fu* by insisting that its descriptions should be grounded on fact, and by eliminating in his work the purely imaginary marvels with which his predecessors were accustomed to embroider their scenes. Tso Ssu's utilitarian and moral purpose did not reduce him to the necessity for firsthand observation, and he was satisfied with the materials which he could cull from written sources. His "Three Capitals" is not as uninspired as his theory implies; his stylistic virtuosity saves it from being merely a guide-book. With Tso Ssu the parallel style has become an inseparable element of *fu* composition.

A further development in the form occurs with the introduction by Yü Hsin (513-581) of a historical theme treated realistically. Within the strict limitations of the extremely artificial style prescribed for the *fu,* Yü Hsin created a great poem about the fall of the Liang dynasty, in which he goes back to the "Li sao" for precedent and introduces himself as a major actor. With his "Lament for the South" (Ai Chiang-nan) the *fu* form reaches its highest development: extreme formalism uniquely combined with a dynamic theme.

Six Dynasties *fu* are predominantly descriptive, the favored topics being natural scenery and meteorological phenomena. At the same time the *fu* was used for portraying emotional states in the *sao* tradition; but the *fu* on separation, homesickness, nostalgia, and the like tend to be impersonal elegiac laments treating the emotion as a formalized abstraction. *Fu* on such themes are usually much shorter than the full-dress descriptive *fu,* and are frequently more to the taste of the Western reader. T'ao Ch'ien's (365-427) "*Fu* on Stilling the Passions" is an adaptation of the elegiac *fu* to the theme of frustrated love; it is a piece filled with elaborate conceits reminiscent of English metaphysical poetry of the seventeenth century.

During the T'ang dynasty the composition of *fu* was turned into an academic exercise by being made a requirement on the civil service examinations. The T'ang *fu* is distinguished from its predecessors by the term "Regulated *fu*" (*lü fu*). The chief innovation was a prescribed rhyme pattern, strict parallelism of lines being already established as essential to the form. A series of four to eight words would be given, usually in the form of a quotation, which had to be used in sequence as rhymes; the topic was also prescribed. *Lü fu* continued to be written as poetic exercises after the T'ang dynasty, but there are no examples of *lü fu* comparable to the earlier *fu* in a freer form.

The tendency toward formalization in the historical development of the *fu* reached its logical climax in the *lü fu*. T'ang poets such as Li Po who wrote *fu* without regard for the new restrictions seldom produced more than variations on themes already exhausted in Han times. Without radical modification the form was finished as a vehicle for poetic expression. The modification appeared in the "O-pang Palace *fu*" of Tu Mu (803-852), with the introduction of a large element of prose, and the more or less haphazard use of rhyme. Ostensibly this was a return to the tradition of the Former Han *fu* writers, but in the hands of the great Sung dynasty poets, Ou-yang Hsiu and Su Shih, the transformation into the new "Prose *fu*" *(wen fu)* was complete. The Prose *fu* is characterized by loose structure, unpredictable rhymes, a judicious use of parallelism, and a strong subjective tone of lyricism reminiscent of the *sao*. It differs chiefly from the Han *fu* in the absence of any moralizing. It is sensuous prose-poetry constructed from the best prosodic elements of the several *fu* forms and allowing the poet the greatest freedom in expressing his ideas; but because of its very formlessness it has been used effectively only by poets of the first rank.

Authorities

Suzuki Torao 鈴木虎雄, "Sōfu no seisei wo ronzu" 騷賦
の生成を論ず, (1924), pp. 321-386 in *Shina bungaku
kenkyū* 支那文學研究.

——————, "Senshin bungaku ni miyuru shōkon" 先秦文學
に見ゆる招魂, pp. 429-445 in *ibid.*

*——————, *Fushi daiyō* 賦史大要 335 pp. (1936).

C. D. Le Gros Clark, *The Prose-Poetry of Su Tung-p'o*, pp. 40-52
(1935) (The best account of the *fu* in English, based in part
on Waley, *The Temple*, pp. 14-18; 58-9).

Translations

I. *Ch'u Tz'u*

1. Li sao

J. Legge, "The Li Sao Poem and its Author," *Journal of
the Royal Asiatic Society* (1895).571-99.
? Lim Boon Keng, *The Li sao, An Elegy on Encountering
Sorrows, by Ch'ü Yüan*, pp. 62-98 (1929).
R. Payne, *The White Pony*, pp. 96-109 (1947).

2. Nine Hymns (Chiu ko)

H. Maspero, "Legendes mythologiques dans le *Chou King*,"
Journal Asiatique 214(1924).21-3 (Tung chün).
A. Waley, *170 Chinese Poems*, pp. 39-40 (Kuo shang)
(1919).
F. Biallas, "K'ü Yüan, his Life and Poems," *JNCBRAS* 54
(1928).248-9 (Tung-huang t'ai-i, Shan kuei).
Payne, *op. cit.*, pp. 81-93 (Tung huang t'ai-i, Yün
chung chün, Hsiang chün, Hsiang fu-jen, Ta ssu-ming,
Shao ssu-ming, Tung chün, Ho po, Shan kuei, Kuo
shang, Li hun).

3. Heavenly Questionings (T'ien wen)

A. Conrady and E. Erkes, *Das älteste Dokument zur
chinesischen Kunstgeschichte: T'ien-wen, die
"Himmelsfragen" des K'ü Yüan* (1928).

4. Nine Declarations (Chiu chang)

Legge, *op. cit.*, 599-600 (Huai sha).

Biallas, *op. cit.*, 241-4 (Hsi yung).

————, "Aus den neun Liedern des K'ü Yüan," *Jubiläums-band,* herausgegeben von der Deutschen Gesellschaft für Natur- und Völkerkunde Ostasiens anlässlich ihrer 60 Jahrigen Bestehens 1873-1933, Tokyo, 1933, Teil 1, 395-409 (Ch'ou-ssu, Huai-sha).

————, "Aus den neun Liedern des K'ü Yüan," *Bulletin No. 9 of the Catholic University of Peking,* 1934, 171-182 (Ssu-mei-jen, Hsi-wang-jih).

————, "Die Letzten der neun Lieder K'ü Yüan's," *Monumenta Serica* 1(1935).138-54 (She chiang, Ai ying, Chü sung, Pei-hui-feng).

Payne, *op. cit.*, pp. 93-95 (She chiang).

5. The Distant Wandering (Yüan yu)

Biallas, "K'üh Yüan's Fahrt in die ferne" *Asia Major* 7(1931).179-241.

6. Determining a Calling by Oracle (Pu chü)

H. Giles, *Gems of Chinese Literature, Prose,* pp. 33-4 (1923).

Biallas, "K'ü Yüan, his Life and Poems," *JNCBRAS* 58 (1928).244-6.

7. The Fisherman (Yü fu)

Biallas, *ibid.,* 246.

8. Nine Persuasions (Chiu pien)

E. von Zach: "Sung Yü's Chiu Pien (Neun Umstimmungen)" uit de *Mededeelingen van het China Instituut,* Batavia, July, 1939, pp. 15-25.

9. The Summons to the Soul (Chao hun)

Erkes, *Das Zurückrufen der Seele (Chao-hun) des Sung Yü* (1914).

10. The Great Summons (Ta chao)

Waley, *More Translations from the Chinese,* pp. 11-19 (1919).

*————, *Chinese Poems*, pp. 36-42 (revised version) (1946).

II. *Fu*

    A. Attributed to Sung Yü (? 3rd c. B.C.)

        1. Big words (Ta yen fu)

        2. Little words (Hsiao yen fu)

        3. Sung Yu's Defense (Feng fu)
            Waley, *The Temple*, pp. 25-27 (1923).

        4. K'ao-t'ang fu
            Waley, *ibid.*, pp. 65-72.

        5. Master Teng-T'u (Teng T'u-tzu hao se fu)
            Waley, *170 Chinese Poems*, pp. 43-4.

        6. The Wind (Feng fu)
            Waley, *ibid.*, pp. 41-2.

        7. The Goddess (Shen-nü fu)
        ? Erkes, "The Song of the Goddess," *T'oung Pao* 25(1928).
            836-402.
            von Zach, *Deutsche Wacht*, June, 1928.

    B. Chia I (B.C. 201-169)

        1. Mourning for Ch'ü Yüan (Tiao Ch'ü Yüan)
            Margouliès, *Le kou-wen chinois*, pp. 66-7 (1925).

    C. Ssu-ma Hsiang-ju (B.C. 179-117)

        1. Tzu-hsü fu
            Waley, *The Temple*, pp. 41-3 (Introduction only).
            von Zach, *Chineesche Revue*, Jan., 1928.

        2. Shang-lin fu
            von Zach, *ibid*.

        3. Ch'ang men fu
            von Zach, *Deutsche Wacht*, Nov., 1928.

        4. The Handsome Man (Mei jen fu)
        ? Margouliès, *Anthologie raisonnée de la littérature chinoise*, pp. 324-326 (1948).

    D. Mei Sheng (d. B.C. 149)

1. Seven Stimuli (Ch'i fa)
    von Zach, *Sinologische Beiträge (SB)* 2.102-5 (1936).

E. Yang Hsiung (B.C. 53-18 A.D.)

1. Driving Away Poverty (Chu pin fu)
    Waley, *The Temple,* pp. 76-80.

2. Kan-ch'uan fu
    von Zach, *Chineesche Revue,* Oct., 1927.

3. Yü-lieh fu
    von Zach, *SB* 2.14-16.

4. Ch'ang-yang fu
    von Zach, *Deutsche Wacht,* Dec., 1928.

F. Pan Ku (32-92)

1. The Two Capitals (Liang tu fu)
    ? Margouliès, *Le "fou" dans le wen siuan,* pp. 31-74 (1925).

2. Yu-t'ung fu
    von Zach, *Deutsche Wacht,* March, 1929.

G. Fu I (?47-92)

1. The Dance (Wu fu)
    von Zach, *ibid.,* Sept., 1928.

H. Pan Chao (d. *ca.* 116)

1. The Great Bird (Ta ch'üeh fu)
2. Needle and Thread (Chen lü fu)
3. Journey to the East (Tung cheng fu)
    Nancy Lee Swann: *Pan Chao: Foremost Woman Scholar of China,* pp. 100-130 (1932).

I. Chang Heng (78-139)

1. The Western Capital (Hsi ching fu)
2. The Eastern Capital (Tung ching fu)
3. The Southern Capital (Nan ching fu)
    von Zach, *SB* 2.1-14.

4. The Skull (K'u-lou fu)
5. Watching the Dance (Kuan wu fu)
    Waley, *The Temple,* pp. 81-6.

6. Ssu-hsüan fu
    von Zach, *Chineesche Revue,* July, 1928.

J. Wang I (?90-after 158)

1. The Lychee tree (Li-chih fu)
    Waley, *The Temple,* p. 87.

K. Wang Yen-shou (?120-?150)

1. Lu-ling-kuang tien fu
    Waley, *The Temple,* pp. 95-7.
    von Zach, *Asia Major* 3(1926).467-90.

2. Wang-sun fu
3. The Nightmare (Meng fu)
    Waley, *ibid.,* pp. 88-94.

L. Wang Ts'an (177-217)

1. On Climbing the Pavilion (Teng lou fu)
    Margouliès, *Le kou-wen chinois,* pp. 110-1.

2. The Widow (Kua-fu fu)
    Margouliès, *Anthologie,* pp. 286-7.

3. The Divorced Wife (Ch'u fu fu)
    Margouliès, *ibid.,* pp. 345-6.

4. Hot Weather (Ta shu fu)
    Margouliès, *ibid.,* p. 358.

M. Ts'ao Chih (192-232)

1. The Spirit of the Lo River (Lo-shen fu)
    von Zach, *Deutsche Wacht,* Aug. 1928.

N. Hsi K'ang (223-262)

1. The Lute (Ch'in fu)
    von Zach, *ibid.,* 1932, No. 10.
    R. van Gulik, *Hsi K'ang and his Poetical Essay on the
    Lute,* pp. 51-70 (1941).

O. Hsiang Hsiu (?225-?300)

1. Ssu-chiu fu
    von Zach, *Deutsche Wacht,* Jan., 1929.

P. Ch'eng-kung Sui (231-273)

1. Whistling (Hsiao fu)
    von Zach, *ibid.*, 1932, No. 4.

Q. Mu Hua (*fl.* 290)

1. The Ocean (Hai fu)
    von Zach, *Chineesche Revue,* Oct., 1929.

R. Chang Hua (232-300)

1. The Tailor-bird (Chiao-liao fu)
    von Zach, *ibid.*, June, 1928.

S. Tso Ssu (? - *ca.* 300)

1. The Capital of Shu (Shu-tu fu)
2. The Capital of Wu (Wu-tu fu)
3. The Capital of Wei (Wei-tu fu)
    von Zach, *SB* 3.134-147.

T. P'an Yo (?-300)

1. Chieh t'ien fu
    von Zach, *Chineesche Revue,* Oct., 1927.

2. Ch'iu hsing fu
    von Zach, *Chineesche Revue,* Oct., 1929.

3. Living in Retirement (Hsien chü fu)
    von Zach, *Deutsche Wacht,* Nov., 1928.

4. Nostalgia (Huai chiu fu)
    von Zach, *ibid.*, Jan., 1929.

5. The Widow (Kua-fu fu)
    von Zach, *ibid.*, Oct., 1928.

U. Lu Chi (261-303)

1. Lament for the Past (T'an shih fu)
    von Zach, *ibid.*, Jan., 1929.

2. On Literature (Wen fu)
    ? Margouliès, *Le "fou" dans le wen siuan,* pp. 81-97.

3. Homesickness (Huai t'u fu)
    ? Margouliès, *Anthologie,* pp. 216-217.

4. Evening (Ta mu fu)
    Margouliès, *ibid.*, pp. 287-288.

5. Winter (Kan shih)
   Margoulies, *ibid.*, p. 258.

V. Kuo P'u (276-324)

   1. The River (Chiang fu)
      von Zach, *Chineesche Revue,* Oct., 1929.

W. Yen Yen-chih (384-456)

   1. Che-pai-ma fu
      von Zach, *Deutsche Wacht,* Apr., 1929.

X. Hsieh Hui-lien (394-439)

   1. Snow (Hsüeh fu)
      von Zach, *Deutsche Wacht,* June, 1928.

Y. T'ao Ch'ien (365-427)

   1. On Stilling the Passions (Hsien ch'ing fu)
      Anna Bernhardi, "Tau Jüan-ming," *MSOS* 15(1912).105-9
      (The introduction to this *fu* is translated in *ibid.*
      18.233-4; *cf.* next entry).

   2. In sympathy with gentlemen not appreciated in their time
      (Kan shih-pu-yü fu)
      A. Bernhardi und E. von Zach, "T'ao Yuan ming," *MSOS*
      18(1915).229-33.

   3. The Return (Kuei-ch'ü-lai tz'u)
      A. Bernhardi, *op. cit.*, pp. 109-112.
      Etudes françaises 3(1941).194-5.
      Payne, *op. cit.*, pp. 170-2.

Z. Pao Chao (421-465)

   1. The Abandoned City (Wu ch'eng fu)
      von Zach, *Deutsche Wacht,* Feb., 1929.

   2. The Dancing Cranes (Wu ho fu)
      von Zach, *ibid.*, July, 1928.

AA. Hsieh Chuang (421-466)

   1. The Moon (Yüeh fu)
      von Zach, *ibid.*, May, 1928.

BB. Chiang Yen (444-505)

1. Separation (Pieh fu)
    ? Margouliès, *Le "fou" dans le wen siuan*, pp. 75-81.

CC. Yü Hsin (513-581)

1. Lament for the South (Ai chiang-nan fu)
    von Zach, *SB* 3.150-6.

DD. Li Po (701-762)
    von Zach, "Lit'aipo's Poetische Werke: I. Buch," *Asia Major* 3(1926).423-66.

III. Regulated *fu (lü fu)*

Su Shih (1037-1101)
    C. D. Le Gros Clark, *The Prose-Poetry of Su Tung-p'o*, pp. 55-8, 70-3, 191-4 (1935).

IV. Prose *fu (wen fu)*

A. Tu Mu (803-852)

1. O-pang kung fu
    Études françaises 4(1943).446-51.

B. Ou-Yang Hsiu (1007-1072)

1. Autumn (Ch'iu sheng fu)
    Waley, *More Translations,* pp. 141-3.

2. The Cicada (Ming ch'an fu)
    Waley, *The Temple,* pp. 99.

C. Su Shih
    Le Gros Clark, *op. cit.,* pp. 81-190, 205-257.

V

PARALLEL PROSE

Parallel Prose *(p'ien-wen)* is characterized by a tendency to use four- and six-word parallel phrases, a somewhat florid and artificial style, an emphasis on verbal parallelism, attention to tonal euphony, occasional rhyme, and frequency of allusion. It is a form of prose that makes use of most of the devices peculiar to Chinese poetry. Parallel Prose flourished during the Six Dynasties, especially during the Ch'i and Liang Dynasties (479-556), going under the name of "Modern Style." The *Anthology (Wen hsüan)* of Hsiao T'ung (501-531) is the great repository of specimens.

The occasional use of parallelism as a rhetorical device in prose is not peculiar to the Chinese language; analogies can be found in most literatures. However, the systematic exploitation of parallelism—as in Lyly's *Euphues*—is usually regarded as an aberration, and unsuited to the nature of the language. Written Chinese, on the other hand, because of its essentially monosyllabic nature, is peculiarly susceptible to constructions where each word in a phrase has its exact counterpart in the succeeding phrase. Examples occur in the most ancient of the Classics, along with such paired, antithetical binomes as heaven/earth, prince/subject, superior/inferior, which themselves invite a more elaborate parallelism. Other purely linguistic factors predispose Chinese to a balanced style. The basic prose rhythm is tetrasyllabic, and even the least mannered prose shows a high occurrence of four-word phrases. When pairs of these are deliberately reduced to a common grammatical pattern the result approaches Parallel Prose. A more subtle kind of rhythm is possible in Chinese, based on the sequence of tones, a phonemic element in the language. Grammatical parallelism, reinforced with strict syllabic correspondence, may be further refined by a similar or contrasting pattern of tones in the parallel phrases. All these elements were probably present in the language of the earliest written documents we know; the development of the style properly called Parallel Prose came about gradually under the influence of several factors which may be divided between literary practice and literary theory.

The chain syllogism so popular with pre-Ch'in philosophical writers provided specimens of sustained parallelism. Its effectiveness as a rhetorical device may have recommended it to writers looking for techniques applicable to literary expression. More certainly influential in the development of Parallel Prose was the practice of the Han writers of *fu*. Many of the characteristics of the style, including the frequency of allusion and the tendency to employ an esoteric vocabulary, are observable in the Han *fu*, but the most important factor was the conscious use of language to achieve artistic effects. Although the consistent use of parallelism in the *fu* hardly antedates the emergence of parallelism in prose, the elaborately artificial diction of Ssu-ma Hsiang-ju has no counterpart in contemporary prose.

Awareness of language as a medium for literature precedes any theorizing about literary technique. Both the awareness and the theory contributed to the technique of Parallel Prose. By the sixth century a distinction was made between belles lettres *(wen)* and utilitarian prose *(pi)*. (The former category also included verse.) Prose, to be literary, apparently had to some extent to be parallel. Since the distinction was based on style rather than on content, any writer with pretentions to literary ability would use the parallel style for all purposes, and would exaggerate the qualities which separated it from the utilitarian. As a result, a full-fledged Parallel Prose became the dominant prose style of the period.

If Parallel Prose is to be defined as more than the use of parallelism in prose, it may be dated from the sixth century, when the new theories of tonal euphony became generally known and were introduced as a necessary factor in elegant prose composition. The style found its most famous practitioners in Hsü Ling (507-583) and Yü Hsin (513-581), who were much imitated, but seldom equalled. Parallel Prose continued to be written through T'ang times, and some of the early T'ang writers—Wang Po (648-675) for example—used the style effectively. But in the hands of less talented writers it tended to be at once mannered and obscure, worthless for literature and ineffectual for practical use. The reaction against Parallel Prose, headed by Han Yü (768-824) and his followers, effected a much-needed reform, but one which was not lasting. It was not until the Sung dynasty that a revived *ku-wen* movement succeeded in replacing Parallel Prose with a more flexible and practical prose. After that, except for chancery documents, Parallel Prose was little practiced until Ch'ing times, when it came into vogue again.

Parallel Prose has been an effective medium for literary production, but only in the hands of a few of the many writers who practiced it. A highly artificial style, it tends to degenerate into a parody of itself when not employed with discretion. It has been used for all kinds of prose composition, including one novel, *(Yen-shan wai-shih),* but is most suited to formal documents and essays.

Authorities

Chin Chü-hsiang 金秬香 , *P'ien-wen kai-lun* 駢文概論, 140 pp. (1934).

Liu Lin-sheng 劉麟生 , *P'ien-wen hsüeh* 駢文學 , 117 pp. (1934).

*—————, *Chung-kuo p'ien-wen shih* 中國駢文史 , 165 pp. (1936).

Translations

E. von Zach, *Sinologische Beiträge* 2.

R. Payne, *The White Pony,* pp. 277-81.

Études françaises 3.5(1942).331-5.

G. Margouliès, *Le kou-wen chinois,* pp. 144-55, 161-6.

VI

LITERARY CRITICISM THROUGH THE SIX DYNASTIES

While occasional passages dealing critically with specific literary works or authors occur as early as Ssu-ma Ch'ien, the beginnings of literary theory come from the Later Han dynasty. The Preface to the *Classic of Songs,* probably by Wei Hung (first century), contains a definition of poetry, "the emotional expression of purposeful thought," and a statement of the didactic function of poetry which was to become a fundamental tenet of what may be called the traditional theory. Another contribution to that theory occurs in the paragraph on *fu* and songs *(shih)* in the *Han shu* "Essay on Bibliography" *(I wen chih),* where these forms are derived from the *Classic of Songs* and judged by their performance as moral allegories or satires in the accepted tradition of the Classic. With the development of a highly artificial style in the *fu* a new element was introduced, the issue between obscurity and clarity, excessive adornment versus simplicity. Wang Ch'ung (27-*ca.* 100) discusses the problem in a chapter of his *Disquisitions (Lun heng),* where in defending his own style he argues for clarity on the grounds that writing, like speech, is for self-expression, a purpose best served by a straightforward style. However he excepts from this generalization the *fu* and the ode *(sung).* Like other Han writers on topics relating to literary theory he has no conception of literature as distinct from writing in general, but is prepared to treat poetry as a special category.

The first work that shows an awareness of literature as an entity is Ts'ao P'ei's (187-226) "Essay on Literature" *(Lun wen),* where he gives summary prescriptions for three prose genres as well as for poetry. While describing the differences between these forms he insists on an element basic to them all, a "spirit" (?) *(ch'i)* underlying all literature. He says nothing about the usefulness of literature, but insists on its value. He deviates from the traditional theory by making the motive for literary composition the enduring fame gained by the writer. The "Essay on Literature" was known to the Six Dynasties theorists, and provides a point of departure for their definitions of genres and speculations about the nature of literature; its greatest influence was perhaps as the first attempt at a systematic evaluation of the work of a series of individual authors.

For all its originality the "Essay on Literature" is, at least in its present form, a badly organized and very sketchy account of its subject. The brilliant "*Fu* on Literature" *(Wen fu)* of Lu Chi (261-303) is a much more sophisticated product. It is at once a description and a demonstration of the process of literary composition. Lu Chi achieves a balanced view of the relative importance of form and content, and postulates the expression of feeling as the motive for writing that is to be considered as literature. He distinguishes ten literary genres, which he characterizes as succinctly as Ts'ao P'ei. In insisting on euphony as a quality of literature he anticipates the theories of the later prosodists and the development of Regulated Verse *(lü-shih)*.

The writings of Lu Chi's contemporaries and successors tended more and more toward excessive verbalism at the expense of content; the artificialities of Parallel Prose and recondite allusion carried Six Dynasties literature beyond the point where it could be reconciled with the traditional theory of its essentially didactic function. By the Liang dynasty (502-556) several important critics attempted either to discredit the tradition or, by restating and elaborating it, to re-establish its authority. The most thoroughly developed canon of literary criticism and theory is Liu Hsieh's (6th century) *Wen-hsin tiao-lung,* an original and effective defense of the tradition. The *Anthology of Literature (Wen hsüan)* compiled by Hsiao T'ung (501-531), friend and patron of Liu Hsieh, was made on principles similar to his. Hsiao T'ung's Preface to his anthology contains a statement of his aims and guiding principles; it is an important document in the history of Chinese literary theory. In opposition to both the traditional theory and contemporary practice, Chung Hung *(fl. ca.* 500) wrote his *Classification of Poets (Shih p'in),* the first systematic attempt at the evaluation of poetry. Representing current, anti-traditionalist views of the nature and function of poetry is the *Yü-t'ai hsin-yung,* an anthology of love poetry compiled by Hsü Ling (507-583) at the command of his patron Hsiao Kang (503-551), younger brother of Hsiao T'ung and heir apparent on the latter's death. (He became the Emperor Chien-wen of the Liang.) The theories represented by this anthology are most clearly stated by Hsiao Kang in two letters, and their discussion will be based on Hsiao Kang rather than Hsü Ling's vague and flowery Preface.

In the background of these several critical theories was the recent formulation of the laws of tonal euphony as stated by Shen Yo (441-513), which were becoming mandatory in poetic composition.

They were accepted by the new school, discussed by Liu Hsieh, and violently rejected by Chung Hung. They are highly relevant to a study of technical prosody but not essential to general theories of poetics and so may be disregarded here. The following is a summary of the critical works mentioned above.

The *Wen-hsin tiao-lung* is a systematized technical discussion of literature, divided into fifty short essays. Its style is Parallel Prose *(p'ien-wen)*, concise to the point of obscurity, loaded with allusions, itself a piece of literature of the first order. The fifty sections are symmetrically divided into two parts, the first half dealing with the origins of forms, the second with the psychological bases of composition. The first four sections contain a general statement of the origin of literature in the Classics, its didactic function as embodying the wisdom of the sages, and the derivation of all existing literary forms from the several Classics. The next twenty-one sections deal with thirty-six forms, proceeding from verse through mixed genres to prose. Genres are established on the basis of function. In each section the terms are defined, the origin of the form determined, its development and modifications considered, and finally the technique of the form discussed in terms of specific examples, which are evaluated. By deriving all existing forms from a Classic, and regarding similar forms as modifications of classical prototypes, Liu Hsieh stretches the classical tradition into a workable hypothesis, though in so doing he frequently has to depend on forced resemblances.

The second half of the *Wen-hsin tiao-lung* begins with a discussion of the creative faculty of the writer, its power and its operations through the inter-related channels of style and character. Styles are divided into eight classes, each of which is adequate for its own purpose, and which reflects the education and ability of the writer. Corresponding to style and character are form and thought, through which the feelings may be expressed adequately. The choice of a proper form calls for an understanding of the changes to which forms are subject; the number of genres is fixed, but they allow of endless variation. If one looks for suitable models, they are not to be found in extremes, but occur where the style is a natural complement of the emotion expressed. Genuine emotion is essential to good writing; decorations must be added to a solid base. It is necessary that the writer have something to say and that he say it well. The proper function of literature is to communicate emotion, not to convince or merely to amaze by a display of verbal virtuosity. Form and expression are the two factors in writing technique subject to control; they may be "molded and cut" according to definite prescriptions.

This completes the discussion in general terms of the nature and technique of literature (seven sections); next are considered in detail various topics of rhetoric and prosody: phonetics, sentence and paragraph divisions, parallelism, metaphor, hyperbole, allusion, vocabulary, (?) connotation (eight sections). The next two sections deal with the principles of literary criticism and the problem of unity. They are followed by a summary and a chronological survey.

The final chapter deals with miscellaneous topics which do not fit into the general scheme of the book: nature as a source of inspiration to the poet, a historical survey of poetic talent, the problem of communication, the effect of a poet's morals on his poetry. The last section is the Introduction, in which Liu Hsieh gives his reasons for writing the *Wen-hsin tiao-lung*.

Hsiao T'ung's *Anthology of Literature* is the largest early collection of pre-T'ang prose and poetry. It has enjoyed enormous prestige in China and has usually provided the basis for the average educated man's knowledge of the literature of the Han and Six Dynasties. Its contents are distributed under three general heads: *fu,* poetry *(shih* and *yüeh-fu),* and prose. The works assembled under the first two are grouped by subject, and arranged chronologically by author. The thirty-seven genres of prose are nearly identical with those of Liu Hsieh, but included are a few that are rhymed and that Liu Hsieh places with the other verse forms. The *Anthology* shows a much more naive grouping than the *Wen-hsin* and lacks any real theoretical basis for distinguishing genres.

The Preface to the *Anthology* contains a statement of the nature of literature, which derives in part from the Wei Hung "Preface to the Classic of Songs," but which admits as literature writings not didactic in purpose and not "derived"—as Liu Hsieh derived them—from any Classic. Without subscribing to the current views of literature, Hsiao T'ung introduces a factor carefully avoided by Liu Hsieh, that of enjoyment. Most of his Preface is concerned, not with theoretical considerations, but with stating his general policy in making selections for the *Anthology*. The Classics are excluded on the grounds that, being perfect, there is no part which can be extracted as better than another. His reason for not making selections from the philosophical writers is that they wrote to express their ideas with no attention to elegance in writing. The stories and speeches in the histories and anecdotal literature are rejected as being too long and readily accessible elsewhere. However, prefaces, commendations and the like, which are short and detachable from their context, he does take from such sources. The various types of documentary prose—memorials, edicts, letters—are well represented.

For all his veneration of the Classics as the highest form of literature and lip-service to the didactic function of literature, Hsiao T'ung in practice makes his selection on the basis of intention, style, appreciation, and finally convenience.

The *Classification of Poets* is a much more specialized work than the above two. Chung Hung limits himself to writers of five-word poetry, which he claims to be the most suitable poetic form. He establishes three degrees of excellence and places all of the 122 poets discussed in one or another of these classes on the basis of "correctness." His criteria for judging are not clearly stated and tend to be subjective. For each poet he asserts a fanciful "derivation" from another poet, presumably implying stylistic similarities, though he may have meant conscious literary influence. The poetry of each writer is characterized in a few words which come to make up the critical vocabulary of later writers on literature; unfortunately they are nearly all metaphorical terms of extreme ambiguity.

Chung Hung's Preface to the *Classification of Poets* is an essay on the derivation of the five-word form and its characteristics. Shen Yo's theory of the four tones is attacked, perhaps through misunderstanding or on personal grounds. Chung Hung is not a traditionalist, but he strongly opposes the excess of his contemporaries in their overly frequent use of allusion and emphasis on the formal aspect of poetry. Like Hsiao T'ung he believes that poetry is emotion elegantly expressed.

Hsü Ling's *Yü-t'ai hsin-yung* is an anthology of love poetry from Han times down to the Liang reflecting the taste and theory of Hsiao Kang, who asserted the independence of literature from the Classics and the inappropriateness of literature as a guide to conduct. His basic precept for poetry is "unrestrained expression of the feelings," his predilection was for the erotic. Under his patronage a group of poets wrote in what came to be known as the Palace Style *(kung-t'i),* which set the tone for subsequent Six Dynasties poetry. It is against this practice that

Liu Hsieh, Hsiao T'ung and Chung Hung were united.

The *Yü-t'ai hsin-yung* contains a good proportion of Palace Style poems, but includes much of the earlier poetry that has in common with the Palace Style only the subject matter. Eight of the ten chapters of the *Yü-t'ai hsin-yung* are devoted to five-word poetry. The ninth chapter is mostly seven-word with a few irregular meters. The tenth has only four-line five-word poems, many of them songs.

Hsü Ling's "Preface," written in purest Parallel Prose, is an elegant eulogy of beautiful women which comes to the point long enough to say that he has made an anthology of love poetry representing a tradition quite distinct from the *Classic of Songs*.

Authorities

*Suzuki Torao, *Shina shiron shi* 支那詩論史 pp. 37-45, 76-109 (1925).

Kuo Shao-yü 郭紹虞, *Chung-kuo wen-hsüeh p'i-p'ing shih* 中國文學批評史 vol. 1, pp. 46-88, 108-140 (1934).

*Aoki Masaru 青木正兒, *Shina bungaku shisō shi* 支那文學思想史 pp. 50-85 (1943).

Chu Tung-jun 朱東潤, *Chung-kuo wen-hsüeh p'i-p'ing shih ta-kang* 大綱, pp. 27-39, 50-74 (1944).

Lo Ken-tse 羅根澤, *Chou-Ch'in liang-Han wen-hsüeh p'i-p'ing shih* 周秦兩漢文學批評史 pp. 87-91, 101-112, 123-140 (1944).

———, *Wei-Chin liu ch'ao wen-hsüeh p'i-p'ing shih* 魏晉六朝文學批評史 pp. 12-15, 24-41, 82-119 (1943).

Translations

1. Wei Hung's "Preface to the *Classic of Songs*"
   J. Legge, *The Chinese Classics* 4 (*The She King*), Prolegomena, pp. 34-36.
   B. Alexéiev, *La littérature chinoise*, pp. 126-27.

2. Lu Chi's *Wen fu*
   ? G. Margouliès, *Le "fou" dans le wen siuan*, pp. 81-97.

3. Hsiao T'ung's "Preface to the *Wen hsüan*"
   ? Margouliès, *op. cit.*, pp. 22-30.
   Alexéiev, *op. cit.*, pp. 31-33.

4. Liu Hsieh's *Wen-hsin tiao-lung*
   Alexéiev, *op. cit.*, pp. 24-27 (extracts from "Yüan tao").
   ? Lim Boon Keng, *The Li sao*, pp. 1-6 ("Pien sao").

VII

CH'U SONGS AND *YÜEH-FU*

The "Nine Hymns" of the *Ch'u tz'u* anthology differ metrically from the *sao* and belong outside the *sao-fu* tradition in that they were intended for a musical setting, if so much may be inferred from their collective title (*ko* = "song"). These hymns, whatever their date, have many Han dynasty parallels, of which the earliest of unquestionable authenticity is the impromptu "Big Wind" song of the first Han Emperor, Kao-tsu. Other similar songs are called "Ch'u songs" in the histories where they are recorded. It is clear that the term refers to the music of the Ch'u region to which the words were sung; however it may be conveniently applied to the song words themselves. The Ch'u song is a true literary genre with definite formal characteristics. Typically such songs use a regular four-, five-, or six-beat line interrupted by a marked caesura. They are usually short (two to twelve lines) and all the early ones purport to be extemporaneous. During the second century and later the form was used for literary imitations which may not all have been intended for musical settings; these tend to be longer than the Former Han specimens. A series of eighteen stanzas by Ts'ai Yen (?162-239?) is the best example of the consciously artistic use of the Ch'u Song and at the same time one of the finest poems in Chinese by a woman poet.

The Ch'u Song makes a convenient bridge between the *sao* and what is known as *yüeh-fu* poetry. It shares with the *sao* the regular use of the particle *hsi*, and like early *yüeh-fu* poems it was originally a song form. The term *yüeh-fu* ("music bureau") is applied to the songs associated with the Bureau of Music established *circa* B.C. 120 by the Emperor Wu and also to poems written in imitation of those songs. In its historical use the term is too inclusive to be described as applying to a well-defined genre; on the other hand, it is too well established to be ignored. After considering the forms covered by the term, it will be possible to restrict its application to song words written within a definite time range.

Music had traditionally been a part of the ritual accompanying sacrifices in the feudal courts of the Chou dynasty; it was likewise assumed also to accompany those poems in the *Classic of Songs* not used for ritual purposes. By Han times the old music had been lost, or at least was found unsuitable to contemporary tastes, if the rare pretenders to a knowledge of classical music really had preserved a few tunes intact. From the time of the founding Emperor, Kao-tsu, popular music consisted of regional folk tunes, of which those of the region of Ch'u were most esteemed; later (in Wu-ti's time) foreign music gained a certain vogue. These seem to have been the only kinds of music available for ritual use. Sanction for such application of popular music was found in the song extemporized to a Ch'u melody by Kao-tsu himself; after his death a chorus was trained to sing the song in his ancestral temple. Wu-ti instituted many new sacrifices, and the demand for ritual songs caused him to found a Bureau of Music charged with the duty of supplying the words, the music, and the orchestration. The tunes were collected from popular sources, or were composed in the manner of the popular tunes; the words were written to order, in each case celebrating the occasion of the ceremony they were to accompany; orchestration was supplied by specialists attached to the Bureau. The Bureau of Music must have been very active; for on its abolition in B.C. 6 there were 829 members to be disposed of. Nearly half of them were assigned to other departments, where they presumably continued their same duties; but the Bureau of Music itself was not reinstituted. In succeeding dynasties the functions of the Bureau of Music were performed by other government agencies, and the texts of some of the songs and hymns which they produced are preserved in the Standard Histories.

A study of these hymns shows them to be archaic in language and meter, stereotyped in content, and of only incidental literary interest. Some are anonymous, others are attributed to known poets. The designation *yüeh-fu* as applied to these song words seems quite apt, implying as it does official sanction and ritual use. However, to avoid confusion with the other category of verse known by the same name, it would be well to specify these as "*yüeh-fu* hymns."

The adaptation to ritual use of an impromptu song by the Emperor Kao-tsu perhaps suggested the extension of the term *yüeh-fu* to other Ch'u Songs improvised by members of the ruling house, or by their protegés. One of them, by the musician and professional entertainer Li Yen-nien (B.C. ? 140-87), is of especial interest as being predominantly in five-word lines, probably the earliest authentic example of the use of this meter for more than a single line.

Aside from these occasional songs, a considerable amount of anonymous ballad literature was preserved in the Imperial Archives, presumably deposited by the Bureau of Music as a by-product of its efforts to collect popular tunes. These collections are known only by their regional titles as recorded in the *Han shu* "Essay on Bibliography," where they occur along with the collections of ritual hymns. It is uncertain whether any survive as the "anonymous old songs" (*yüeh-fu ku-tz'u*) of the later anthologies, though some of the latter must date at least from the Later Han period (25-220). It is likely that some of these song words were used, along with their original tunes, on official occasions. The Bureau of Music provided not only ritual hymns, but music for all official functions. That included military songs and music for receptions and banquets. The latter, especially, did not necessarily require subject matter appropriate to the specific occasion, and the entertainers could have sung popular sentimental ballads for the amusement of the guests. Such a practice would explain the preservation of the love songs, the complaints of abandoned wives, of returned soldiers, of neglected orphans that today are taken as the forerunners of Chinese lyric poetry. This early ballad literature is much more intimately a part of the poetic tradition than the not dissimilar poems of the *Classic of Songs*, by virtue of its use of a more modern form of the language: most of these songs must have been quite intelligible to the ear.

Excepting the hymns, post-Han *yüeh-fu* are not predominantly song words. Han music was displaced by other types, some of them foreign importations, and the old tunes were lost. The lack of a tune did not prevent later poets from imitating *yüeh-fu* songs which had survived as lyric poems, and such imitations were customarily given the name of the original song. What was imitated was usually the subject or the mood, not the prosodic form, and the imitations are for the most part in five-word verse. In T'ang times the imitations were of the style or manner, Po Chü-i in particular employing the irregular versification characteristic of the early *yüeh-fu* for his "New *yüeh-fu*," in which he followed neither title, subject nor specific form but used the old ballads as an excuse for writing free verse. At the same time song words were written to existing tunes, and these too would be called *yüeh-fu*, though in no way connected with the activities of the long defunct Bureau of Music. They could be in regular five-word meter, or in the free meters more characteristic of the Han ballads.

The term *yüeh-fu* could be usefully restricted to (a) the early (? Han dynasty) ballads, (b) imitations of those ballads, when written to be sung, (c) song words written to new tunes in the

51

ballad tradition. This would exclude five-word poetry written under a *yüeh-fu* song title but with no musical setting and not intended to be sung. It would admit the T'ang imitations only under the classification of New *yüeh-fu*, useful in that it indicates their direct inspiration but keeps them distinct as non-musical compositions. It excludes song forms (*chüeh-chü*, *tz'u, ch'ü*) which supplanted the *yüeh-fu* and which produced other distinguishable verse types.

Authorities

*Suzuki Torao, "Kan-mu no gakufu to saigai kakyoku" 漢武の樂府と塞外歌曲 (1910), *Shina bungaku kenkyū*, pp. 42-54.

Lu K'an-ju 陸侃如, *Yüeh-fu ku-tz'u k'ao* 樂府古辭考 pp. 1-11 (1926).

*Lo Ken-tse 羅根澤, *Yüeh-fu wen-hsüeh shih* 樂府文學史, 290 pp. (1931).

————, "Ho wei yüeh-fu chi yüeh-fu ti ch'i-yüan" 何謂樂府及樂府的起源, *An-hui ta-hsüeh yüeh-k'an* 安徽大學月刊 2.1(1934).40 pp.

Hsiao Ti-fei 蕭滌非, *Han Wei liu-ch'ao yüeh-fu wen-hsüeh shih* 漢魏六朝樂府文學史 pp. 1-146 (1933/1944).

Translations

I. Ch'u Songs

    1. Ching K'o (B.C. ?-227)
       Derk Bodde, *Statesman, Patriot and General in Ancient China*, pp. 23-38 (1940).

    2. Hsiang Yü (B.C. 232-202)
       E. Chavannes, *Les mémoires historiques de Se-ma Ts'ien* 2.316(1895).

    3. Liu Pang (Han Kao-tsu) (B.C. 248-195)
       Homer Dubs, *The History of the Former Han Dynasty* 1. 136-7(1938).

    4. Liu Ch'e (Han Wu-ti) (B.C. 157-88)
       Waley, *170*, p. 69.

    5. Li Ling (B.C. ?-74)
       Waley, *170*, p. 74.

    6. Liu Hsi-chün (B.C. ?140-87?)
       Waley, *170*, p. 75.

    7. Hsü Shu (*ca.* 147)
       Waley, *170*, p. 77.

II. *Yüeh-fu*

   A. *Yüeh-fu* hymns

      E. von Zach; *Sinologische Beiträge* 2.67(1935).
    ? G. Margouliès, *Anthologie raisonée de la littérature chinoise,* p. 368 (1948).
      D. von den Steinen, "Poems of Ts'ao Ts'ao," *Monumenta Serica* 4(1939).140-2, 151-3, 157-8, 159-60, 162-3, 170-1, 174-5.

   B. Early anonymous *yüeh-fu*

      Waley, *170,* pp. 45-58, 71-2, 74(2), 122-6.
      von Zach, *SB* 2.67-8.
      Lectures chinoises 1(1945).104.
      R. Payne, *The White Pony,* pp. 126-30 (1947).

   C. *Yüeh-fu* songs by known authors

    1. Ts'ao Ts'ao (155-220)
      von Zach, *SB* 2.68-9.
      Stefan Balazs, "Ts'ao Ts'ao, zwei Lieder," *MS* 2(1937). 418-20.
      D. von den Steinen, *op. cit.,* pp. 130-1, 134, 136, 137-8, 144-5, 147-8, 154-5, 166-7, 176-80.

    2. Ts'ao P'ei (188-226)
      von Zach, *SB* 2.69.

    3. Ts'ao Chih (192-232)
      von Zach, *SB* 2.69-70.

    4. Miao Hsi (?-245)
      Waley, *170,* p. 99.
      von Zach, *SB* 2.73.

    5. Fu Hsüan (217-278)
      Waley, *170,* pp. 93-4.
      Margouliès, *Anthologie,* pp. 312, 336.

    6. Lu Chi (261-303)
      von Zach, *SB* 2.73; *Deutsche Wacht* 1932.23-4.
      Margouliès, *Anthologie,* pp. 298-9, 389, 431.

    7. T'ao Ch'ien (365-427)
      Anna Bernhardi, "Tau Jüan-ming," *MSOS* 15(1912).81-5.
      von Zach, *SB* 2.73-4.

    8. Hsieh Ling-yün (385-433)
      von Zach, *SB* 2.62, 70-1.

9. Yüan Shu (408-453)
   von Zach, *SB* 2.93-4.

10. Pao Chao (421-465)
   von Zach, *SB* 2.71-3.
   ? Margouliès, *Anthologie*, pp. 336-8, 390-1.

11. Hsieh T'iao (464-499)
   Waley, *170*, p. 128.
   von Zach, *SB* 2.73.

12. Lu Chüeh (472-499)
   von Zach, *SB* 2.74.

13. Fan Yün (451-503)
   Margouliès, *Anthologie*, p. 313.

14. Yang Kuang (569-618)
   Waley, *170*, p. 139.

D. New *yüeh-fu*

   1. Po Chü-i (772-846)
      Waley, *170*, pp. 180, 183, 188, 192-200.
      Payne, *op. cit.*, pp. 264-6, 271-2.

III. Pre-T'ang five-word poetry (*shih*)

A. The "Nineteen Old Poems"
   Waley, *170*, pp. 59-68.
   von Zach, *SB* 2.74-6.
   Études françaises 2(1940).716-20, 774-8; 3(1941).55-8,
   122-5.

B. "Li Ling-Su Wu" poems
   Waley, *170*, pp. 73-4.
   von Zach, *SB* 2.77.

C. "Southeast the Peacock Flies" (a *yüeh-fu* ballad?)
   Waley, *The Temple*, pp. 113-25.
   Études françaises, 6(1941).477-93.
   Ayscough, *Chinese Women, Yesterday and Today*, pp. 250-
   62.

D. Chronologically by authors

   1. K'ung Jung (153-208)
      Lectures chinoises 1(1945).106.
      Giles, *Gems of Chinese Literature, Verse*, p. 34.

   2. Wang Ts'an (177-217)

von Zach, *SB* 2.20, 26, 39, 66-7, 78.
Margouliès, *Anthologie,* pp. 227, 274.

3. Liu Cheng (?-217)
   von Zach, *SB* 2.20, 43-4, 78.

4. Ying Ch'ang (?-217)
   von Zach, *SB* 2.20.

5. Hsü Kan (171-218)
   ? Giles, *Gems,* p. 36.

6. Ts'ao P'ei (188-226)
   Waley, *170,* p. 85(2).
   von Zach, *SB* 2.32, 78.

7. Ts'ao Chih (192-232)
   Waley, *170,* pp. 85 (1) (correct "Wei Wen-ti" to "Ts'ao
   Chih")-89, 132 (correct "Wu-ti").
   von Zach, *SB* 2.19-20, 24-6, 39, 44-5, 79-80; *Deutsche
   Wacht* 1933.5.

8. Ying Chü (190-252)
   von Zach, *SB* 2.29-30.

9. Hsi K'ang (223-262)
   von Zach, *SB* 2.80.

10. Juan Chi (210-263)
    von Zach, *DW* 1932.7.
    Waley, *170,* p. 91.
    Margouliès, *Anthologie,* pp. 432-4.
    Payne, *op. cit.,* pp. 147-8.

11. Ch'eng Hsiao (?220-?264)
    Waley, *170,* p. 83.

12. Fu Hsüan (217-278)
    von Zach, *SB* 2.80.
    Waley, *170,* pp. 93-4.

13. Chang Tsai (*ca.* 285)
    von Zach, *SB* 2.39, 91.
    Waley, *170,* pp. 97-8.

14. Tsao Chü (*ca.* 285)

von Zach, *SB* 2.81.

15. Wang Tsan (*ca.* 290)
    von Zach, *SB* 2.81.

16. Sun Ch'u (?-293)
    von Zach, *SB* 2.25.

17. Fu Hsien (239-294)
    von Zach, *SB* 2.51.

18. Kuo T'ai-chi (?239-?294)
    von Zach, *SB* 2.51.

19. Chang Hsieh (*ca.* 295)
    von Zach, *SB* 2.27-28, 82-83.

20. Wang Sung (3rd c.)
    Waley, *170,* p. 90.

21. Chang Hua (232-300)
    von Zach, *SB* 2.46, 80.
    Margouliès, *Anthologie,* p. 228.

22. P'an Yo (?-300)
    von Zach, *SB* 2.25, 40, 58-9.

23. Ou-Yang Chien (?-300)
    von Zach, *SB* 2.38.

24. Tso Ssu (*ca.* 300)
    Waley, *170,* pp. 95-6.
    von Zach, *SB* 2.26-7, 31, 81-2.

25. Ho Shao (?-301)
    von Zach, *SB* 2.30, 46, 81.

26. Lu Chi (261-303)
    von Zach, *SB* 2.31, 48-9, 60, 80, 89-91.
    Margouliès, *Anthologie,* pp. 276-7, 368.

27. Lu Yün (262-303)
    von Zach, *SB* 2.51-2.

28. Ssu-ma Piao (?-306)
    von Zach, *SB* 2.45-6.

29. Ts'ao Shu (?-308)
    von Zach, *SB* 2.80-1.

30. P'an Ni (?-310)
    von Zach, *SB* 2.59-60.

31. Liu K'un (270-317)
    von Zach, *DW* 1932.9.

32. Chang Han (?258-?319)
    von Zach, *SB* 2.82.

33. Kuo P'u (276-324)
    von Zach, *SB* 2.30-1.

34. Lu Ch'en (284-350)
    von Zach, *SB* 2.28, 52-3, 83.

35. Hsieh Tao-yün (*ca.* 376)
    Waley, *170,* p. 120.

36. Chan Fang-sheng (*ca.* 400)
    Waley, *170,* p. 121.

37. Yin Chung-wen (?-407)
    von Zach, *SB* 2.32.

38. Hsieh Hun (*ca.* 412)
    von Zach, *SB* 2.32.

39. Hsieh Chan (387-421)
    von Zach, *SB* 2.25, 28, 53.

40. T'ao Ch'ien (365-427)
    Anna Bernhardi, "Tau Jüan-ming," *MSOS* 15(1912).79-81,
        85-105, 115-7.
    —————————and E. von Zach, "T'ao Yüan-ming," *MSOS*
        18(1918).189-228.
    yon Zach, *SB* 2.60-1, 84, 91.
    Etudes françaises 2.2(1940).184-8.
    Waley, *170,* pp. 103-114.
    R. Payne, *op. cit.,* pp. 156-170.

41. Hsieh Ling-yün (385-433)
    von Zach, *SB* 2.17-18, 22, 25-6, 32-4, 40-1, 54-5, 61-3.

42. Hsieh Hui-lien (394-430)

von Zach, *SB* 2.32, 37, 53-4, 84.

43. Fan Yeh (398-445)
    von Zach, *SB* 2.22.

44. Liu Shuo (431-453)
    von Zach, *SB* 2.94.

45. Yen Yen-chih (384-456)
    von Zach, *SB* 2.29, 34-5, 41, 55-6, 64.

46. Wang Seng-ta (423-458)
    von Zach, *SB* 2.56, 94.

47. Pao Chao (421-465)
    Waley, *170,* pp. 129-31.
    von Zach, *SB* 2.29, 35-6, 64, 86, 94-5.

48. Hsieh T'iao (464-499)
    von Zach, *SB* 2.36, 41, 56-7, 64-5, 86-7.
    Margouliès, *Anthologie,* p. 434.

49. Lu Chüeh (472-499)
    von Zach, *SB* 2.57-8.

50. Fan Yün (451-503)
    von Zach, *SB* 2.58, 95.

51. Chiang Yen (444-505)
    Giles, *Gems,* p. 49.
    von Zach, *SB* 2.36, 65, 95-102.

52. Jen Fang (460-508)
    von Zach, *SB* 2.41-2, 58.

53. Ch'iu Ch'ih (464-508)
    von Zach, *SB* 2.24, 65-6.

54. Yü Hsi (*ca.* 510)
    von Zach, *SB* 2.29.

55. Shen Yo (441-513)
    Waley, *170,* p. 131.
    von Zach, *SB* 2.24, 36-7, 66, 88-9.

56. Hsü Fei (?-525)
    von Zach, *SB* 2.37.

57. Hsiao Kang (504-552)
    Waley, *170,* p. 133.

58. Hsiao I (508-554)
    Waley, *170,* p. 135.

59. Hsü Ling (507-583)
    Waley, *170,* p. 138.

60. Yü Hsin (513-581)
    von Zach, *SB* 3.156-9.

VIII

FIVE-WORD AND SEVEN-WORD POETRY

Before the Han dynasty, poetry *(shih)* was normally written in four-word lines. Occasional aberrant lines occur in the *Classic of Songs* and elsewhere, but the five-word line was not used as a regular meter throughout a poem. The *sao* form frequently varied its usual six-word line to include lines shorter or longer, but it showed no tendency to develop a regular five-beat measure. The emergence toward the end of the Han dynasty of the five-word line *(wu yen)*, which for several centuries was almost the only *shih* meter, has led literary historians since the sixth century to look for its origins in what has been preserved of the older poetry. The search, complicated and misled by unreliable dating and attributions, is probably misdirected effort: a literary form is in its nature an abstraction which begins to exist as writers recognize distinguishing features in specific literary works and consciously shape their own writings to conform to those features. If the problem of origins is restated as a search for antecedents, these can be found for the five-word poem in certain subliterary compositions, the "common sayings" and prophetic "boys' songs" recorded in the *History of the Former Han Dynasty*. These are for the most part doggerel verses, of which the earliest datable example in lines of five words comes from the time of Wu-ti (B.C. 140-87). There are enough verses of this type to indicate their widespread occurrence. The earliest attempts to use the five-word line for literary poetry are probably lost beyond recovery, though the feeble "Historical Poem" (Yung shih shih) attributed to Pan Ku, may be an example.

During the last half of the second century the five-word line was used for literary poetry of considerable merit, if any of the attributions to Ch'in Chia (*ca.* 150), K'ung Jung (153-208), or Wang Ts'an (177-217) are reliable.

In these poems are found all the prosodic features normal to the developed five-word form. Rhyme is at the end of alternate lines, and each line has a light caesura after the second beat, superimposing a 2:3 rhythm on the five-beat line. It is this rhythmic counterpoint which is responsible for the preference given by Chinese poets to this line over any of the earlier measures in which Chinese poetry had been written. Characteristically each line is end-stopped and forms an independent grammatical unit. Run-on lines do occur, especially in poetry of the second and third centuries, but as the form developed the tendency was to make each line a self-contained unit, a tendency reinforced by the growing use of strict grammatical parallelism between paired lines.

In the third century the five-word form was the medium for an efflorescence of lyric poetry which began in the court of the Wei ruler Ts'ao Ts'ao (155-220); his son Ts'ao Chih (192-232) was the first major poet to make extensive use of the new form. Five-word poetry remained the dominant *shih* form until the T'ang dynasty, when it was rivaled but not displaced by the seven-word line; its history during the intervening Six Dynasties is a history of Six Dynasties poetry. Even the *yüeh-fu* (except for *yüeh-fu* hymns) tended to become regularized into five-word verse. In this period the most important poet was T'ao Ch'ien.

Seven-word poetry *(ch'i yen shih)* appeared as a distinct genre much later than the five-word form, though isolated examples are found from the second century, such as Chang Heng's "Four-fold Sorrow" (Ssu ch'ou shih). This poem, however, was written in the *sao* tradition, as the author clearly stated in his preface, and no more than the coda *(luan)* to his *fu* "Meditation on Mystery" (Ssu hsüan fu), also in regular seven-word lines, it is a typical example of the seven-word form. A *yüeh-fu* poem by Ts'ao Chih is in seven-word lines, but like Chang Heng's it uses rhyme at the end of each line instead of the alternate rhymes standard in five-word and true seven-word poetry. Poems analogous to these were occasionally produced throughout the Six Dynasties period, but only toward the sixth century are there seven-word poems with alternate rhyme and a regular caesura after the fourth beat characteristic of the developed form.

The early examples by Chang Heng and Ts'ao Chih suggest possible antecedents for the form. The *sao* line was often in a seven-beat measure, and *yüeh-fu* songs also employed occasional long lines. More relevant is the very common practice in Han times of casting congratulatory wishes, popular sayings, and especially mirror inscriptions in seven-word rhymed verse. These are as early as the first century B.C., and their widespread popularity may have influenced the practice of literary poets. It was only after the five-word poem had been well established that the seven-word form became a recognized genre; probably it was shaped into a facsimile of the already accepted form.

Seven-word verse came into its own during the T'ang dynasty.

The longer line offered more possibilities than the five-word form, especially in the restricted *lü-shih* and *chüeh-chü* stanzas. It was used by all the major T'ang poets, and in later periods remained of equal importance with the five-word line.

Authorities

Suzuki Torao, "Gogen shi hassei no jiki ni taisuru gimon" 五言詩發生の時期に對する疑問 (1919), *Shina bungaku kenkyū*, pp. 22-41.

_____, "Hakuryōdai no renku" 柏梁台の聯句 (1911), *ibid.*, pp. 55-73.

Lo Ken-tse, "Ch'i yen shih chih ch'i-yüan chi ch'i ch'eng-shu" 七言詩之起源及其成熟, *Shih-ta yüeh-k'an* 師大月刊 2(Jan. 1933).24-58.

Lu Ch'in-li 逯欽立, "Han shih pieh lu" 漢詩別錄, *CYYY* 13(1948).269-334.

Translations

I. Pre-T'ang five-word poetry (see pp. 55-60)

II. Pre-T'ang seven-word poetry

    1. Chang Heng (78-139)
       von Zach, *SB* 2.77-8.

    2. Ts'ao P'ei (188-226)
       von Zach, *SB* 2.69.

    3. Lu Chi (261-303)
       von Zach, *SB* 2.91.

IX

LÜ-SHIH

Regulated Verse *(lü-shih)* is the term applied to poetry written in five- or seven-word lines, with an eight-line stanza, following a prescribed and invariable rhyme-scheme, and observing strict rules of verbal parallelism and tonal sequence in certain lines. It is a verse form which, like Parallel Prose, also deliberately exploits all the prosodic features of the language. The rules defining *lü-shih* were formulated late in the seventh century, on the basis of what had become accepted practice in versification.

The beginnings of *lü-shih* go back to the fifth century, when the four tones of the Chinese language were first named and their function in prosody defined by Shen Yo (441-513) and others. Before that time the effect of the tones on euphony and rhythm no doubt influenced the practice of versification, if only on an unconscious level, but Shen Yo's "eight defects" supplied a formula that could be used to control these factors even where a poet's ear might fail to warn him. Each of the "eight defects" describes in metaphorical language a possible flaw in versification. Only four of them relate directly to tonal euphony, the "defects" consisting in the use of two words with identical tones in certain homologous positions in a line or couplet. Shen Yo's prescriptions were not universally observed or accepted without controversy. Poetry had been written in the past, and continued to be written, in violation of the rules. But they were not forgotten, and in time two of them came to be accepted as a necessary part of the *lü-shih* stanza.

Tone was also a factor involved in rhyme. Perfect rhyme in Chinese requires that the rhyming words be of the same tone, but imperfect rhymes were frequent in earlier poetry, especially in the *yüeh-fu*. *Lü-shih* demanded perfect rhymes, and further restricted all rhyming words to one of the four possible tones.

The almost universal practice of Parallel Prose during the sixth and seventh centuries undoubtedly influenced verse forms, and the *lü-shih* rules, as a codification of practice, included a requirement for parallelism between the lines of two couplets of poems written as Regulated Verse.

The rules governing Regulated Verse can best be summarized for the five-word line; the seven-word form is analogous but rather more complicated. In considering the rules it should be remembered that they were originally generalizations based on actual practice, that both rules and practice were concerned with euphony, and that exceptions to and violations of the rules are common, especially among the great T'ang poets. The restrictions based on tones are the most typical of the *lü-shih* forms, and may be dealt with first. For prosodic purposes the four tones are divided into two categories, level and deflected. An uninterrupted sequence of words in either of the tone-categories is difficult to pronounce, as a series of spondees would be, and is usually avoided in Chinese poetry, even that which would not qualify as Regulated Verse. There the rule requires that the second and fourth words of a five-word line be of different tone (i.e., tone-categories), and a corollary forbids the use of identical tones in the last three words of a line. These rules effectively prevent such a difficult sequence, since the five-word line is divided after the second word by a caesura, and for prosodic purposes the two parts may be treated separately. There is another minor rule dealing with the occurence of tones within a single line, the avoidance of a single level tone word between two with deflected tones. For the five-word form this rule applies only to the final three words; it is frequently violated in the seven-word form.

The eight lines of a *lü-shih* poem are treated as a series of couplets, the tone pattern of one line determining that of the paired line. The rule requires the second word of each initial line to have a different tone from the same word in the next line; but the words in that position in the second and first lines respectively of adjacent couplets must be of the same tone.

Verbal and grammatical parallelism may occur between the two lines of each couplet; it is prescribed for the second and third couplets.

Rhymes must appear in the second, fourth, sixth, and eighth line; exceptionally the first line may also carry a rhyme (it does so regularly in the seven-word form). The rhyme-words must all be of level tone, and the same rhyme is carried throughout the poem.

Further rules apply to the development of an idea in the *lü-shih* and the repetition of words. These rules are extremely scholastic, and are so often violated that their validity is questionable. All the rules are applicable only to Regulated Verse; verse which did not follow the rules was known as "old style" *(ku-shih)* in contrast to "Modern Style" *(chin-t'i)* or

Regulated Verse.

A variant of *lü-shih* was *p'ai lü,* verse of undetermined length (up to several hundred lines) which observed most of the rules of Regulated Verse, but was allowed to vary the rhyme. Candidates were required to write a specimen *p'ai lü* on the civil service examinations during the T'ang period.

It was during the T'ang period that *lü shih* first appeared as a recognized verse form. In the hands of Tu Fu (712-770) this very exacting form became the vehicle for lyric and occasional verse of unsurpassed beauty and vigor. No other Chinese poet of his stature was so consistently able to make the conventions of the form serve the ends of poetical expression. *Lü shih* occupies a prominent part in the works of nearly all the major T'ang poets and ever since has been a part of the stock in trade of every practicing poet.

Lü shih tends to be held in low esteem today. The decline of poetry (*shih*) after the T'ang is attributed to the dominance of this form, and in a sense the accusation is valid, since the process of linguistic change altered the tones and made the T'ang rhymes no longer accurate to the ears of later poets who were nevertheless bound to use them in writing Regulated Verse. *Lü-shih* prosody had ceased to be functional. At the best only a great poet could observe the multiple restrictions of *lü-shih* and still write poetry. But by observing the rules, any educated person could produce the semblance of poetry in *lü-shih*, and in a society that put a premium on ability at versification, it was inevitable that it should be practiced by every aspirant. It was in this form that students and beginners were trained, and it is not surprising that many writers of little talent grew up thinking they were poets because of their facility in writing in a difficult verse form.

Authorities

A. Waley, "Notes on Chinese Prosody," *JRAS* 1918, pp. 249-261.

Kiang Kang-hu, "Various poetic regulations and forms," *The Jade Mountain,* Introduction, pp. xxviii-xxxv.

Liu Ta-pai 劉大白 , "Chung-kuo chiu shih chung ti sheng-tiao wen-t'i," 中國舊詩中的聲調問題 , 60 pp. in *Chung-kuo wen-hsüeh yen-chiu* 中國文學研究 (1927).

——————, "Shuo chung-kuo shih-p'ien chung ti tz'u-ti lü" 說中國詩篇中的次第律 , 14 pp. in *ibid.*

Shionoya On 鹽谷温, *Shina bungaku gairon kōwa* 支那文學概論講話, pp. 93-107 (1928).

Aoki Masaru 青木正兒 , *Shina bungaku gaisetsu* 支那文學概説, pp. 97-104 (1935).

Translations

A. Waley, *170 Chinese Poems,* pp. 153-5, 163, 205, 216, 224, 227, 229, 243.
——————, *More Translations,* pp. 32-3, 78-9, 81, 83, 90, 92, 97, 128.

S. Obata, *The Works of Li Po,* pp. 44, 51, 90, 96, 105, 111, 156-7, 193 (1922).

X

CHÜEH-CHÜ

Chüeh-chü, literally "broken-off lines" is a term applied to five- or seven-word verses consisting of only four lines. Originally in the fifth and sixth centuries it was used to designate short song stanzas, and so constituted a sort of *yüeh-fu* with no formal restrictions implied other than line and stanza length. In T'ang times the *chüeh-chü* continued to be associated with musical settings, but it also developed as an independent verse form subject to some of the rules governing Regulated Verse. In the latter version it became the most sophisticated and exigent of all Chinese verse forms. The twenty words of a five-word *chüeh-chü* were expected to carry the matter and weight of a *lü-shih* verse twice its length. Conciseness and concentration were achieved by reliance on connotation and allusion. The characteristic *chüeh-chü* of T'ang times may be defined as a four-line verse which with the greatest economy of words is used to express emotion, describe a scene or recall an event by selecting the essential segment or aspect of the subject. Economy of words is prescribed by the form, which leaves no room for padding or verbiage; each word must contribute to the effect of the whole poem. The best examples hold in suspension several levels of meaning, and more than for other poetry, a prose paraphrase would run to many times the length of the original. The limitation of length makes it impossible to achieve effects by accumulating details; the *chüeh-chü* must contain the distilled essence of its subject, but in such a way that only relevant details will be suggested to the reader. The art of the *chüeh-chü* is one of suggestion, but the effect must be clear-cut; there is no place for overtones that distract from its dominant tone. The form is suitable for lyric subjects, not for narrative. Allusion and word-plays are devices frequently used to achieve the requisite compression.

The difficulty of the *chüeh-chü* form is increased by the observance of the restrictions proper to Regulated Verse, especially the alternation of tones (level and deflected) in the lines of each couplet. The rule is not as binding in *chüeh-chü,* but is usually followed. The prescribed rhyme scheme is also similar to that of *lü-shih,* but rhyme words with deflected tone are admitted in the first line of the seven-word form. There is not the same tendency for the lines of a *chüeh-chü* to be grouped in couplets, and the *lü-shih* rules of parallelism do not apply, though parallelism of a subtler kind is observable in many *chüeh-chü.*

Elaborate rules, analogous to those for *lü-shih,* were formulated defining the function of each of the four lines of a *chüeh-chü,* whereby the first line should establish the theme, the second continue it, the third introduce a "turn," a new element, and the fourth resolve all into a harmonious whole. These rules were made long after the T'ang poets had furnished the classical examples of the form, and are at the most only descriptive of tendencies, being violated in many of the best *chüeh-chū.* The basic fact underlying them is the relative independence of each of the four lines; run-on lines do not occur. And it is true that the third line tends to be the critical one.

Chüeh-chü were written by all the major poets of the T'ang and Sung dynasties. Wang Wei (699-750), Li Po (699-762), Wang Ch'ang-ling (*fl.* 726), Su Shih (1036-1101), and Huang T'ing-chien (1045-1105) are the most important poets in this form. Like *lü-shih, chüeh-chü* continued to be written up to modern times, but few outstanding examples occur after the Sung dynasty.

Authorities

Suzuki Torao, "Zekku sogen" 絶句遡源 (1921), pp. 157-72
　　Shina bungaku kenkyū.

Hung Wei-fa 洪為法, *Chüeh-chü lun* 絶句論, 102 pp. (1934).

Translations

A. Waley, *Chinese Poems,* pp. 115, 116-7, 125, 150-1, 186, 197
　　(1946).

Bynner and Kiang, *The Jade Mountain,* pp. 3, 4, 10-17, 20, 24-6,
　　28, 36, 45, 52-5, 73-5, 86-7, 89, 94-5, 97, 100, 103-4, 108,
　　116-8, 136, 141, 142, 146-7, 175-8, 180-1, 184-6, 189-91,
　　205-6, 213, 215.

R. Payne, *The White Pony,* pp. 179-82, 194, 196, 200-7, 210-13,
　　266, 267, 269, 271, 273, 274, 282, 284, 285, 286, 287, 288,
　　291, 292, 305, 319-21, 322, 325, 351, 353, 361, 365, 366, 367,
　　368, 370-2, 373.

XI

THE *KU-WEN* MOVEMENT

The elaborate Parallel Prose style which had developed during
the Six Dynasties continued to be almost universally practiced
during the first two centuries of the T'ang dynasty. However, its
inadequacy as a vehicle for effective communication had been
recognized by the first Emperor of the Sui dynasty, who made an
unsuccessful attempt to prevent its use in chancery documents.
Occasionally T'ang dynasty writers raised objections to the style
on aesthetic or ethical grounds and advocated a return to pre-Han
models of free prose. The practical difficulty of using Parallel
Prose for extended narrative led the early T'ang historians to
abandon it in their work. Some of them expressed dissatisfaction
with the style as decadent and unsuited to the properly didactic
function of literature. The reaction developed into a full-
fledged literary movement with political and philosophical overtones under the leadership of Han Yü (768-824), whose writings are
at once the prototype and the model for the reformed prose known
as *ku-wen* (Ancient Style, in contrast to the current Parallel
Style).

Ku-wen prose as written by Han Yü and his followers drew its
inspiration from pre-Han models of expository prose and certain
Han writers of history and narrative. However, it was not
confined to a slavish imitation of those models, either in
vocabulary or syntax. Like its models, *ku-wen* obeys no arbitrary
rules of prosody; it is a true prose, with prose rhythms and only
occasional adventitious ornaments of the sort that characterized
Parallel Prose. At the same time it is an artificial style in the
sense that even in T'ang times it was not derived from a living
colloquial language; still, it was probably influenced by the
spoken language to some extent. Giving considerable scope for
individual expression, it revived the moribund essay and provided
a medium for fiction, a genre that had developed little since Han
times.

That *ku-wen* was accepted for a time as a serious competitor
of Parallel Prose was only in part because of a recognition of its
merits. It found in Han Yü an advocate who was also an effective
propagandist. Known as a Confucian, a moralist and a staunch
conservative, he was in a position to damn with authority the
"new style" prose along with the other heresies, native or imported,

of Taoism and Buddhism. For Han Yü *ku-wen* was only a part of a program, if an essential part, concerned with reforming the times by a return to antiquity, a revival of the way of Confucius as transmitted through Mencius. He set himself up as a teacher in the Confucian tradition, attracted disciples, and founded a school. Except among the Buddhists, such a procedure was not common in his time, and gave impetus to his movement. The success of the *ku-wen* movement was closely connected with the T'ang examination system for the selection of civil service candidates. Candidates were expected to write an essay in Parallel Prose, and were judged by their skill in observing the complicated rules of such composition. As education was designed to qualify students for the examinations, the emphasis was on the study of models of Parallel Prose style rather than on broad reading or even on the Confucian Classics. Critics of the system insisted that it resulted in the selection of officials who were unqualified by learning or moral character—both developed only by a close study of the Classics—for responsible positions. Such criticisms gained point during the disastrous rebellion of An Lu-shan at the end of the eighth century, when it was easy to assume that the civil war was the direct result of incompetency and corruption in officialdom. Han Yü's strong belief in education in Confucian morality supported his advocacy of a prose style based on the writings of the early Confucians, and those in charge of the examinations were prepared to consider candidates who were trained in Han Yü's school and who wrote *ku-wen* prose.

Han Yü's attitude toward literature was essentially a restatement of the traditional theory, with its insistence on the primarily didactic function of all writing. Suspicious of art as artificiality, he insisted that prose should be straightforward and unadorned. Since he valued content above manner, there should be no place in his aesthetic canon for frivolity. But *ku-wen* prose was a suitable vehicle for narration as well as for exposition, and the writers of tales and anecdotes turned *ku-wen* to their own uses, which were not always edifying to a Confucian moralist. After Han Yü's death the chief practitioners of the style he had tried to popularize were the authors of such tales, especially toward the end of the dynasty when a revival of Parallel Prose displaced *ku-wen* for official and serious use.

In Sung times the conflict between the two styles again became an issue, with Han Yü the patron saint of the *ku-wen* advocates. A series of outstanding literary men, starting with Ou-yang Hsiu

(1007-1072), devoted themselves to the theory and practice of *ku-wen,* with the result that Parallel Prose was finally displaced in all categories of writing except the documentary. The position of *ku-wen* as the only acceptable prose style was not again challenged until early Ch'ing times when *p'ien-t'i* was revived by a school of writers headed by Chang Hui-yen, and even then *ku-wen* maintained its dominance.

Authorities

Cheng Chen-to, *Chung-kuo wen-hsüeh shih,* pp. 478-91 (1932).

Ch'en Chu 陳柱, *Chung-kuo san-wen shih* 中國散文史 , pp. 191-264 (1937).

Kung Shu-chih 龔書熾, *Han yü chi ch'i ku-wen yün-tung* 韓愈 及其古文運動, 124 pp. (1945).

Liu K'ai-jung 劉開榮 , *T'ang-tai hsiao-shuo yen-chiu* 唐代 小說研究 , pp. 1-23 (1947).

Yoshikawa Kōjirō 吉川幸次郎 , *Tōdai no shi to sambun* 唐 代の詩と散文 , pp. 53-73 (1948).

Translations

H. A. Giles, *Genus of Chinese Literature, Prose,* pp. 115-96, 202-30, 241-50, 260-76.

G. Margouliès, *Le kou-wen chinois,* pp. 177-230, 242-351.

FICTION IN THE LITERARY LANGUAGE

Fiction in the literary language developed little from the Han to the T'ang, when the *ch'uan-ch'i* (tale of the marvelous) appeared as a new genre. Six Dynasties tales and anecdotes provided some of the themes and techniques for the T'ang *ch'uan-ch'i,* and though they are not comparable to the earlier thematic elaborations of legend and history found in such works as the *Tso chuan,* they are more immediately the inspiration for T'ang fiction. There are six collections of anecdotes centering about the court of the Emperor Wu of the Han, ostensibly historical works devoted to historical figures and attributed to known writers of the Han period; actually they contain much more of legend and hearsay than sober history, and are certainly not the product of their putative authors, men like Pan Ku and Liu Hsin. These books, of which the *Miscellaneous Notes on the Western Capital (Hsi-ching tsa-chi)* is perhaps the best known, borrow their organization and form from the annals or monograph sections of the histories of Ssu-ma Ch'ien and Pan Ku. Their often lurid accounts of what went on inside the court were probably intended to pass as an inside history, not as historical fiction.

Collections of humorous anecdotes appear to have been popular during the Six Dynasties. Only one survives in its original form, the *New Specimens of Contemporary Talk (Shih-shuo hsin-yü)* by Liu I-ch'ing (403-444). This book reflects in a series of short anecdotes and conversations the current of nihilism and pessimism that spread through the intellectual world with the decay and collapse of the Han dynasty in the third century. The sophistical "Pure Talk" *(ch'ing t'an)* appearing in some of these conversations is the earliest example of what might be called wit in Chinese. *Contemporary Talk* is written in a mannered prose, chiefly in the form of dialogue.

Several collections of tales of the supernatural survive from Six Dynasties times. The *Sou shen chi* by Kan Pao (*ca.* 300) may be taken as representative. In it brief accounts of marvels are presented as records of actual occurrences; the purpose of the collection was to edify, not to amuse. The tales are of considerable interest to the student of folklore, but they show a rudimentary narrative technique. Some of the themes and anecdotes elaborated in the T'ang *ch'uan-ch'i* occur in this and other similar collections of the same period.

Aside from the numerous translations of Buddhist canonical works made during the Six Dynasties period a derivative native literature of Buddhist sermons and apologues appeared in China before the T'ang dynasty. They are all religious in inspiration and intent but are used to illustrate such ideas as the working of karma through metempsychosis, the efficacy of the sutras, and the magical powers of the Buddhist clergy; they are not concerned with subtleties of doctrinal theology, and so were of interest to a wider audience than the professionally religious. From these apologues are derived a group of *ch'uan-ch'i* tales.

In T'ang times the tale reached its maturity as a literary form. The various earlier types provided themes and contributed to the narrative technique of the *ch'uan-chi*, but the stimulus for the production of this more sophisticated narrative came from factors new to Chinese society. One factor was the new prose medium—*ku-wen*—promoted by Han Yü and his followers. Six Dynasties tales were written in a more free prose than the prevalent *p'ien-wen*, but the lack of prestige of such prose must have hampered the development of narrative style. The early T'ang tale in *p'ien-wen* that has survived, the *Visit to the House of Beauties (Yu hsien k'u)*, shows the inadequacy of Parallel Prose for narration. It is significant that the great development and widespread popularity of the *ch'uan-ch'i* coincides with the rise of the *ku-wen* movement.

The practice of having candidates for the civil service examinations submit to their examiners a "practice composition" *(wen-chüan)* in which they were to demonstrate their ability at narration, exposition, and versification has been linked with the contemporary development of the *ch'uan-ch'i*, as these tales frequently contain the three elements. Such a demand would certainly lead to the widespread practice of this type of composition as preparation for acceptance on the examinations, and successful candidates as well as those who failed might have continued to write stories for amusement even after the practical demand had ceased to apply.

Another stimulus was provided by the relative position of the three religious systems during the T'ang. Buddhism had by then become a part of Chinese culture, Taoism had revived under imperial patronage, and Confucianism found supporters of the caliber of Han Yü among the bureaucracy. Advocates of all three used the tale as a vehicle for supporting their own claims and for exposing the pretentions of their competitors. The supernatural machinery and setting common to many tales of the marvelous were derived from the currently accepted picture of heaven and hell and their inhabitants as described by the Buddhists and Taoists.

The bulk of T'ang fiction in the literary language can be conveniently described as belonging to five categories. Of these, the fictional biographies of historical persons were a direct continuation of the Han tradition, and like their prototype were cast in a form imitating the biographies in the Standard Histories. They deal with contemporary T'ang figures, chiefly poets or the more notorious of the imperial concubines. These sketches show no great technical advance over their predecessors, and probably should not be considered as *ch'uan-ch'i* tales.

Also with Han prototypes are the few T'ang hero stories, but these reflect a very different attitude toward their subject. The adventures of the hero are no longer bound to follow a prescribed ritual pattern. His motivation may be chivalrous or capricious; there is not the undercurrent of predetermined fate that characterizes the earlier hero story. The intrusion of the supernatural or marvelous appears as a fortuitous ornament rather than as a token of divine concern with the hero's fate.

The religious *ch'uan-ch'i* tales are more elaborate than the Six Dynasties apologues and through better characterization have greater interest as stories. The moral is less obtrusive, even in the tales retold from earlier versions. Both Taoism and Buddhism provide the materials for *ch'uan ch'i* tales; in addition there are many stories containing attacks on the clergy and beliefs of the two religions. Among the stories that depend on Buddhist or Taoist cosmology for their setting are those which use the other world as a vehicle for social criticism. Since the world of the dead is a faithful replica of this world in its social organization, abuses and inequalities could be safely attacked by describing the corrupt and bungling administration of the spirit world.

The most remarkable group of *ch'uan-ch'i* tales is that of love stories. There was no precedent in T'ang times for love as a subject for fiction. Mildly erotic accounts of the relationship of emperors and favorite concubines were known—the *Fei-yen wai chuan* is an example—but no tales of romantic attachment. The T'ang love stories are the most realistic of the *ch'uan-ch'i* and depend less on supernatural agencies for the working out of their plots. The love affairs described sometimes involve girls of good family, but more often the girl is either a courtesan or a fox-fairy. The connections are nearly all illicit; only exceptionally is the love of a married couple the subject for a story. It is probable that the sudden appearance of this new topic in fiction reflects a changed status of women in Chinese society, possibly as a result of the reign of the T'ang Empress Wu. The brothels which flourished in the capitals and commercial centers, providing an opportunity for men to meet educated and attractive young women, were also a factor in popularizing romantic attachments that could provide material for stories. At least one of these tales (the *Hui chen chi*) is known to be autobiographical, and it is likely that others had a basis in fact or current gossip.

Besides the preceding categories of tales there are a large number which can be classified only as tales of the marvelous, a description which applies as well to all of T'ang *ch'uan-ch'i*. The unusual phenomena or events which are recorded may belong to the supernatural, describing feats of magic, the behavior of witches, and the fulfillment of omens, or brief paragraphs instructing the reader in dragon lore; these all are subjects which had appeared in the Standard Histories since Han times, and which were undoubtedly accepted as factual even out of such context. Other, more elaborate tales deal with unusual situations of everyday life: exemplary behavior, devoted friends, eccentric people. For these too precedent existed in Han and Six Dynasties stories, especially in the *Lieh nü chuan* and the *Shih-shuo hsin-yü*.

Literary language fiction flourished in T'ang times, but found few practitioners during the Sung. Hung Mai's *I chien chih* is a large miscellaneous collection of historical notes and anecdotes, but not ostensibly fictional. The large collection of post-Han fiction, the *T'ai-p'ing kuang-chi*, was made at the order of the Sung Emperor T'ai-tsung. In it are preserved most of the surviving T'ang *ch'uan-ch'i*. Further collections were made in Ming times, when a new interest in the form is shown by Ch'ü Yu's stories of the marvelous, the *Chien teng lu* and the *Chien teng hsin hua*, imitated after T'ang models. In these collections love stories predominate, with an element of erotocism verging on the pornographic.

The great revival of the *ch'uan-ch'i* form came in the Ch'ing dynasty. The most famous is the *Liao-chai chih-i (Strange Stories)* of P'u Sung-ling (1640-1715), unexcelled in style and general literary excellence. The range of subject matter in the 431 stories comprising the *Liao-chai* is identical with that of the earlier *ch'uan-ch'i;* in fact some of the same plots re-appear. But P'u Sung-ling achieves a new degree of realism in treating the supernatural and writes in a style at once simple and elegant that vitalizes the flimsiest and most hackneyed plots.

The literary language has also been used as a medium for full-length novels, but none of them are comparable with the great popular language novels. The *Yen-shan wai-shih* of Ch'en Ch'iu (*ca.* 1850) is a novel of over 300,000 words in Parallel Prose style based on a Ming *ch'uan-ch'i* tale. The plot is absurd and the style so involved and mannered as to require a commentary. A *ku-wen* novel, the *Yin shih* by T'u Shen (1744-1801) is in part an imitation of the vernacular novels *Hsi yu chi* and *Feng-shen yen-i.* The large element of magic places it also in the *ch'uan-ch'i* tradition.

Authorities

Derk Bodde, "Some Chinese Tales of the Supernatural: Kan Pao and his *Sou-shên chi*," *HJAS* 6(1942).338-44.

Ch'en Yin-k'o, "Han Yü and the T'ang novel," *HJAS* 1(1936).39-43.

E. D. Edwards, *Chinese Prose Literature of the T'ang Period,* vol. 2, pp. 1-34 (1938).

Wang Chung-han, "The Authorship of the Yu-hsien-k'u," *HJAS* 11 (1948).153-62.

W. Eberhard, *Die chinesische novelle des 17.-19. Jahrhunderts (Artibus Asiae,* suppl. 9) 239 pp. (1948).

Liu K'ai-jung, *T'ang-tai hsiao-shuo yen-chiu,* pp. 1-152.

Cheng Chen-to, *Chung-kuo wen-hsueh shih,* pp. 492-511.

T'an Cheng-pi 譚正璧 , *Chung-kuo hsiao-shuo fa-ta shih* 中國 小說發達史 , pp. 137-206 (1934).

Kuo Chien-i 郭箴一 , *Chung-kuo hsiao-shuo shih,* vol. 1, pp. 122-60 (1939).

Translations

I. Fictionalized History

    1. *Han Wu-ti ku-shih*

        "Histoire anecdotique et fabuleuse de l'Empereur Wou des Han," *Lectures chinoises* 1(1945).28-91.

    2. *Fei-yen wai-chuan*

        Lin Yutang, *The Wisdom of China and India,* pp. 956-63 (1942).

    3. *Tung ming chi*

        "Tong-fang Chou," *Études françaises* 4(1943).64-6 (Excerpt translated by Chen Pao-Ki [Shen Pao-chi]).
        Lionel Giles, *A Gallery of Chinese Immortals, (Wisdom of the East Series)* p. 17 (1948).

II. Anecdote and Humor

    1. *Shih-shuo hsin-yü*

        Werner Eichhorn, "Zur chinesischen Kulturgeschichte des 3. und 4. Jahrhunderts," *Zeitschrift der deutschen Morgenländischen Gesellschaft* 91(1937).462-80.

        R. H. van Gulik, *Hsi K'ang and his Poetical Essay on the Lute,* p. 22 (1941).

III. Tales of the Supernatural

    1. *Sou shen chi*

        D. Bodde, "Some Chinese Tales of the Supernatural," *HJAS* 6(1941).344-55.

        Lin Yutang, *op. cit.,* pp. 946-7.

        L. Giles, *op. cit.,* pp. 50, 76-8, 88-90, 93-4.

        W. P. Yetts, "Taoist Tales," *New China Review* 1(1919). 170.

    2. *Sou shen hou-chi*

        W. P. Yetts, *ibid.,* 171-4.

    3. *Shih-i chi*

        "Deux Anecdotes," tr. by Tchang Lomine (Chang Jo-ming), *Études françaises* 4(1943).220-3.

    4. *Lieh hsien chuan*

        L. Giles, *op. cit.,* pp. 17-21, 22-6, 27-31, 34-6, 45-7, 50-5, 62-4, 67-8, 79-81, 95-6, 105-6.

        W. P. Yetts, *ibid.,* 12-5.

    5. *Shen hsien chuan*

        L. Giles, *op. cit.,* pp. 21-2, 31-3, 38-41, 42-5, 55-61, 64-7, 83-5, 90-2, 95-7.

IV. *Ch'uan-ch'i*

  A. T'ang

    *1. E. D. Edwards, *Chinese Prose Literature of the T'ang Period,* vol. 2, pp. 35-410 (Translations, summaries and notes from the fictional material in the *T'ang-tai ts'ung-shu).*

*2. Chi-chen Wang, *Traditional Chinese Tales*, pp. 1-114
   (1944).

3. "Histoire de la courtesane Li," tr. by Pao Wen-wei, *Études
   françaises* 4(1943).382-94, 459-72.

4. "Histoire de Dame Saule," tr. by Schlemmer and Li Hi-tsou,
   ibid., 4(1943).128-37.

5. "Histoire de Tou Tse-tch'ouen," tr. by Kermadec and Kao
   Ming-k'ai, *ibid.*, 3(1942).607-715.

B. Post-T'ang

1. "Histoire de Tong Hsiao-wan," tr. by Kermadec and Kao
   Ming-k'ai, *Études françaises* 4(1943).282-97.

2. Herbert Giles, *Strange Stories from a Chinese Studio,*
   488 pp. (Bowdlerized translations of 164 stories from
   Liao-chai chih-i) (1916).

3. Rose Quong, *Chinese Ghost and Love Stories,* 329 pp.
   (Translations from *Liao-chai*) (1946).

4. W. Eberhard, "Aus Yüan Me 'Der Meister sagte nicht...'
   (Dsi pu yü)," *Sinica* 11(1936).50-2.

XIII

SCHOOLS OF SUNG POETRY

Although the Sung dynasty produced at least as much poetry as the T'ang, Sung poetry is on the whole inferior in quality. Symptomatic of an unmistakable decline in creativeness in the traditional *shih* forms was the disposition of Sung poets to form literary schools and cliques. Only the major poets of the period remained relatively independent. The existence of schools of poetry affords a convenient guide to the chief Sung dynasty poetic canons and facilitates the treatment of the host of versifiers who wrote the great bulk of Sung poetry.

Chronologically the earliest, the Hsi-k'un school, was a continuation and intensification of late T'ang and Five Dynasties practice. Yang I (974-1020) and Liu Yün (*fl.* 1016) were the leaders of the Hsi-k'un school; their works are marred by preciosity, over-refined technique, elaborate allusions, and stereotyped themes. All the Sung schools took one or more T'ang poets as models; the Hsi-k'un chose for theirs the late T'ang poet Li Shang-yin.

The inevitable reaction against the inadequacies of Hsi-k'un poetry was led by Ou-yang Hsiu, famous also as the restorer of *ku-wen* prose. Together with Su Shun-ch'in (1008-1048) and Mei Yao-ch'en (1002-1060) he wrote poetry modeled after that of Han Yü, whence the name Ch'ang-li School. Their poetry, though in a sense derivative, marked a great advance over that of the Hsi-k'un poets and put a quick end to the existence of that school.

The Ch'ang-li school did not survive beyond the generation of poets who founded it, but like the *ku-wen* movement which they also sponsored, it effected a break with the decadence of early Sung writing and prepared the way for a group of really outstanding poets. Wang An-shih (1026-1070), Su Shih (1036-1101), and Huang T'ing-chien (1045-1105) wrote most of the best poetry of the Northern Sung period. None of them adhered to any preexisting school, and though all had disciples and followers, only Huang T'ing-chien left a clearly enunciated set of poetic principles which could be taken as the program for a school of poetry. His poetry is marked by the use of allusion, the range of which extended even beyond the sources ordinarily used by the more erudite poets. His practice led him to the generalization that every word in the poetry of his favorite models, Tu Fu and Han

84

Yü, had its specific source, and that a poet could do no better than follow their precept.

The Chiang-hsi School was so called from the name of Huang T'ing-chien's native region; its members made every attempt to write in accordance with his principle. Characteristically they took poetry seriously and devoted themselves to perfecting a poetic technique. The strength and viability of the school was derived from the fact that it offered a stringent technical training, and while only the versifiers remained loyal to the circumscribed view of poetry dictated by the school, it was in it that all later Sung poets of any stature served their apprenticeship. The only important poet who wrote consistently in the Chiang-hsi manner was Ch'en Shih-tao, who achieved apparent ease and naturalness in his poetry only by dint of the most painstaking effort. Ch'en Yü-i (1090-1137), Yang Wan-li (1124-1206), Lu Yu (1125-1209), and Fan Ch'eng-ta (1126-1193) all began their careers as Chiang-hsi poets, and are nominally associated with the school, but each of them repudiated the school and developed an individual style.

The reaction against the Chiang-hsi school led to the formation of another school, the Ssu-ling, whose four (ssu) original members all chose pen-names with the word ling as a component. They and their followers were active during the period 1190-1243, concentrating on such technical details as the two parallel couplets in five-word lü shih, a concern that betrays Chiang-hsi influence, while rejecting the Chiang-hsi practice of allusion. Their poetry at its best is restrained and lucid, but much of it is insipid and pointless. Chao Shih-hsiu (?-1219) is the best known of the Ssu-ling poets; Hsü Chao (?-1211), Hsü Chi (1162-1214), and Weng Chüan (ca. 1205) are the three others who founded the school.

The Chiang-hu ("Rivers and Lakes") School is a convenient cover name for over a hundred late Sung poets who had little in common except a distaste or incapacity for an official career. Some of them were acquaintances, but they evolved no poetic theory or program. They tended to accept both Chiang-hsi and Ssu-ling models, writing in the manner of both. Only two Chiang-hu poets are important: Chiang K'uei (1155-1208) and Liu K'o-chuang (1187-1269), both of whom are better known as writers of tz'u.

The remaining school is that of the moral Philosophers (Li hsüeh). Philosophy attracted some of the best minds among Sung writers, and contaminated much of Sung poetry. Its worst effects

are to be seen in the poetry written by the philosophers themselves. Their attitude toward poetry was either disapproving
or utilitarian, and their verses for the most part are moralizing
doggerel. Shao Yung (1011-1077) is the only one of them with
any gift for poetry, though the most famous, Chu Hsi (1130-1200),
left quantities of mediocre verse among his voluminous literary,
philosophical, and critical works.

Authorities

Hu Yün-i 胡雲翼, *Sung shih yen-chiu* 宋詩研究, 240 pp. (1930).

K'o Tun-po 柯敦伯, *Sung wen-hsüeh shih* 宋文學史, pp. 85-124 (1934).

Liang K'un 梁崑, *Sung-shih p'ai-pieh lun* 宋詩派別論, 175 pp. (1938).

Translations

I. Poets Associated with Schools

    A. Ch'ang-li School

        1. Mei Yao-ch'en (1002-1060)

            A. Forke, *Dichtungen der T'ang- und Sung-Zeit*, pp. 107-9 (1929).

            G. Margouliès, *Anthologie raisonnée de la littérature chinoise*, pp. 282, 301-3, 343, 355, 381, 393, 441.

        2. Shih Chieh (1005-1045)

            Forke, *Dichtungen*, p. 119.

        3. Ou-yang Hsiu (1007-1072)

            Forke, *Dichtungen*, pp. 110-15.

            Margouliès, *Anthologie*, pp. 194, 292, 376-8, 439.

        4. Su Shun-ch'in (1008-1048)

            Forke, *Dichtungen*, p. 117.

            Margouliès, *Anthologie*, pp. 303, 417.

    B. Chiang-hsi School

        1. Huang T'ing-chien (1045-1105)

            Forke, *Dichtungen*, pp. 157-8.

             Margouliès, *Anthologie*, p. 235.

        2. Liu Tzu-hui (1101-1147)

            Margouliès, *Anthologie*, p. 381.

        3. Yang Wan-li (1124-1206)

            Forke, *Dichtungen*, pp. 159-62.

             Margouliès, *Anthologie*, pp. 196, 235, 381, 442.

        4. Lu Yu (1125-1210)

            A. Waley, *170 Chinese Poems*, pp. 153-5.

            Forke, *Dichtungen*, pp. 163-4.

Clara Candlin, *The Rapier of Lu: Patriot Poet of China*, 68 pp. (1946).

Margouliès, *Anthologie*, pp. 235, 282, 393, 394, 442.

5. Fan Ch'eng-ta (1126-1193)
Forke, *Dichtungen*, pp. 166-7.
Gerald Bullett, *The Golden Year of Fan Cheng-ta*, 44 pp. (1946).
Margouliès, *Anthologie*, pp. 195, 234.

C. Ssu-ling School

1. Hsü Chao (d. 1211)
Margouliès, *Anthologie*, pp. 197, 282.

2. Weng Chüan (*fl.* 1205)
Margouliès, *Anthologie*, pp. 304, 381.

D. Chiang-hu School

1. Ch'en Tsao (1133-1203)
Margouliès, *Anthologie*, p. 194.

2. Liu K'o-chuang (1187-1269)
Margouliès, *Anthologie*, p. 235.

3. Tai Fu-ku (*fl.* 1200)
Forke, *Dichtungen*, pp. 169-72.
Margouliès, *Anthologie*, p. 417.

4. Fang Yo (1199-1262)
Margouliès, *Anthologie*, p. 255.

E. Li-hsüeh School

1. Chu Hsi (1130-1200)
Forke, *Dichtungen*, pp. 167-8.
Margouliès, *Anthologie*, p. 234.

II. Independent Poets

1. Hsü Hsüan (916-991)
Forke, *Dichtungen*, p. 105.
Margouliès, *Anthologie*, pp. 355, 439.

2. Wang Yü-ch'eng (954-1001)
Forke, *Dichtungen*, p. 106.

3. Han Ch'i (1008-1075)
Forke, *Dichtungen*, p. 118.

4. Chao Pien (1008-1084)
Margouliès, *Anthologie*, p. 379.

5. Wang An-shih (1021-1086)
   Forke, *Dichtungen*, pp. 121-5.
   H. R. Williamson, *Wang An Shih*, 1.11-2, 14, 15, 16, 20,
       21, 27-8, 40-1; 2.291-2.
   Margouliès, *Anthologie*, pp. 233, 254, 380.

6. Wang Ling (1032-1095)
   Forke, *Dichtungen*, pp. 126-8.

7. Su Shih (1036-1101)
   Waley, *170 Chinese Poems*, p. 151.
   Forke, *Dichtungen*, pp. 128-47.
   H. H. Hu and Harold Acton, "Nine Poems of Su Tung-p'o,"
       T'ien Hsia Monthly 8(1939).181-9.
   Lin Yutang, *The Gay Genius*, pp. 45, 47, 50-1, 52-3, 58,
       138, 139-40, 141, 142, 145, 146, 148-9, 151, 155,
       162, 165, 166-7, 168, 169, 170, 171, 172, 174, 175,
       185-6, 199, 200, 204, 215, 218, 226, 285, 297, 360,
       367 (1947).
   Margouliès, *Anthologie*, pp. 379, 439, 440.

8. K'ung Wen-chung (1038-1088)
   Forke, *Dichtungen*, p. 149.

9. K'ung Wu-chung (1041-1097)
   Forke, *Dichtungen*, p. 148.

·10. K'ung P'ing-chung (*fl.* 1085)
   Forke, *Dichtungen*, pp. 149-52.

11. Ch'in Kuan (1049-1100)
   Forke, *Dichtungen*, p. 156.
   Margouliès, *Anthologie*, pp. 234, 380-1, 441.

12. Chang Lei (1052-1112)
   Forke, *Dichtungen*, pp. 153-5.

13. Ch'ao Pu-chih (1053-1110)
   Forke, *Dichtungen*, p. 158.

14. Ch'ao Kung-su (*fl.* 1150)
   Margouliès, *Anthologie*, p. 235.

15. Yeh Shih (1150-1223)
   Forke, *Dichtungen*, p. 169.

16. Tai Ping (*fl.* 1230)
   Margouliès, *Anthologie*, p. 197.

17. Wen T'ien-hsiang (1236-1282)
   Forke, *Dichtungen*, p. 172.

XIV

TZ'U

The *tz'u* is a song-form characterized by lines of unequal length, prescribed rhyme and tonal sequences, occurring in a large number of variant patterns, each of which bears the name of a musical air. The vocabulary of the *tz'u* admits colloquial language elements not common in the *shih*. It is analogous both to the earlier song-form *yüeh-fu* and to the *ch'ü* which appeared later. The *tz'u* was evolved during the T'ang dynasty. It was the only poetic form successfully practiced during the succeeding Five Dynasties, and during the Sung was the vehicle for much of the best poetry, competing with older *shih* forms in popularity but carrying less prestige. The most productive period of the *tz'u* was from the early tenth through the twelfth centuries. *Tz'u* continued to be written into modern times, but as purely literary verse; its function as song was taken over by the *ch'ü*.

Poetry with unequal lines is as old as the *Classic of Songs;* examples occur in the *Ch'u tz'u* and among the Han dynasty *yüeh-fu,* where they are definitely associated with musical settings. That poets of the T'ang period could be influenced by such precedents, even in a time when the regular *shih* forms were the norm, is shown by such irregular non-musical compositions as Li Po's *"Ku feng"* and Po Chu-i's "New *yüeh-fu."* Poets occasionally took liberties with even such exigent forms as the *chüeh-chü* and *lü-shih;* examples occur of seven-word *chüeh-chü* with one or more six-word lines. Such a variation is possible without destroying the dominant rhythm established by a seven-word line which, because of the caesura, carries eight beats. A six-word line, when recited, fits the same rhythm, the third and sixth words each accounting for two beats. Thus length of line in a given regular verse form is not invariable, even in the absence of the demands of musical phrasing.

However, *tz'u* is intimately bound up with music. T'ang dynasty popular tunes were for the most part foreign importations coming from Central Asia and elsewhere. Song words for such tunes could be supplied in three ways: a pre-existing poem could be adapted to a given tune, a new poem could be written in a traditional form for the tune, or a new poem could be written directly for the tune and derive its form from the musical phrasing peculiar to that tune. The last alternative would produce the multitude of

patterns characteristic of the *tz'u,* and was undoubtedly responsible for the examples of the form once established. But there
is good evidence that poems in the strict *lü-shih* and *chüeh-chü*
forms, especially the latter, were sung to the foreign tunes.
Even assuming that no syllable-to-note correspondence was possible
or attempted in such cases, there must have been discrepancies
between musical phrase and poetic line that could be reconciled
only by supplying refrain, meaningless syllables or the like.
Traces of such devices appear frequently in the earliest acknowledged *tz'u,* and the practice is attested by Sung dynasty writers
on the subject. As the demand for song words in standard verse
forms weakened, greater freedom could be taken with line length,
meaningful words being written in a given line wherever the music
required vocalization, regardless of the resulting violation of
the underlying *lü-shih* or *chüeh-chü* form. Subsequently song words
would conform to no other requirement than harmony with the musical
setting; but for a given tune, the beats and phrasing being fixed,
any song words would follow the same pattern. This pattern
extended, with some possibility of variation, to the tone of each
word in a line. The resulting pattern, known by the name of the
tune underlying it, came to be regarded as a definite verse form,
and as such was utilized by poets who wrote in ignorance of the
original melody. The preservation of the melodies themselves was
difficult because of the lack of an adequate system of notation,
but any *tz'u*—song words for a tune—served to establish a pattern
that could be followed.

The surviving *tz'u* patterns bear the titles of T'ang and Sung
dynasty songs. However, not all of them are based directly on
those songs. As the *tz'u* form became established, it underwent
certain modifications and complications. New patterns were made,
so that longer *tz'u* could be written, thus extending the possible
range of subject matter of the *tz'u,* in its early form chiefly
limited to lyrical themes, especially love.

The earliest school of *tz'u* writers is known by the name of
the Five Dynasties anthology *Hua-chien chi.* It contains highly
sophisticated love poetry by late T'ang and early Five Dynasties
poets, who lived in the western state of Shu (Szuchuan) written
in a manner reminiscent of the Liang dynasty Palace Style. The
poet given the greatest amount of space in the anthology is Wen
T'ing-yün (*fl.* 860), who is usually taken as representative of
the *Hua-chien* school. His *tz'u* are subtle, voluptuous, and
suggestive; their weakness is an over-refinement that implies

91

shallowness of feeling.

The same objection does not apply to Li Yü (937-978), who combines as great a technical skill with a poignant lyricism found only in the greatest of the Chinese poets. Li Yü, as an eastern poet, is not represented in the *Hua-chien chi,* and because of the individual quality of his genius, was not a poet subject to imitation. Consequently his influence on the Sung dynasty *tz'u* writers was less than that of the *Hua-chien* school.

The *tz'u* form is usually associated with the Sung dynasty. It was then that most of the famous *tz'u* poets lived, and the form reached the height of its popularity. At the beginning of the dynasty the *Hua-chien* influence was dominant, especially in the work of Liu Yung (*fl.* 1045), who stuck to the *Hua-chien* themes but wrote for a popular audience. His fame was rivaled only by that of the poet Su Shih (1036-1101), who used the *tz'u* form for non-lyric subjects and tended to violate the prescribed patterns. With him the *tz'u* begins to be divorced from music and to become a purely literary verse form. He is considered to be the founder of a "school"; his followers were those who wrote *tz'u* on other than erotic topics. The Southern Sung *tz'u* poets include adherents of both schools; Hsin Ch'i-chi (1140-1207) belonged to Su Shih's school by virtue of his subject matter. He used a greater admixture of colloquial language in his *tz'u* than his contemporaries. Many of the older *tz'u* melodies had been lost by Southern Sung times, but new tunes continued to be composed. Chiang K'uei (?1150-?1230), a musician, composed new melodies for his *tz'u,* written in a literary style.

After the Sung dynasty there is only one *tz'u* poet comparable to these writers, Na-lan Hsing-te (1655-1685), a Manchu. His *tz'u* are chiefly love poems, some of them in new patterns.

Authorities

Suzuki Torao, "Shigen" 詞源, *Shina bungaku kenkyū,* pp. 459-78 (1922).

Aoki Masaru, "Shikaku no chōtanku hattatsu no gen'in ni oite" 詞格の長短句發達の原因に就て , *Shina bungei ronsō* 支那文藝論叢 pp. 67-85 (1923).

Lung Mu-hsün 龍沐勛 , "Tz'u-t'i chih yen-chin" 詞體之演進 , *Tz'u-hsüeh chi-k'an* 詞學季刊 1(1933).1-44.

Glen Baxter, "Metrical Origins of the *Tz'u,*" HJAS 15(1952).

Translations

? Clara M. Candlin, *The Herald Wind: Translations of Sung Dynasty Poems, Lyrics and Songs, (Wisdom of the East Series),* pp. 31-113 (1933).

*Ch'u Ta-kao, *Chinese Lyrics,* 54 pp. (1937).

Teresa Li, "Fourteen Chinese Poems," *T'ien Hsia Monthly* 6(1938).82.
_____, "Poems from the Chinese," *ibid.,* 239-41, 245.
_____, "Fifty-six Poems from the Chinese," *TH* 8(1939).78-89, 93, 96-7, 98.
_____, "Fifty Poems from the Chinese," *TH* 8(1939).292-327, 329.

N. L. Smith and R. H. Kotewall, "Twenty-four Chinese Poems," *TH* 9(1939).388-9, 392, 396-7, 399.

Feng Shu-lan, *La technique et l'histoire de ts'eu, thèse pour le Doctorat de l'Université de Paris,* 175 pp. (1935).

Wang Soo-ying, *Na-lan Sing-to, thèse pour le Doctorat de l'Université...de Paris,* 92 pp. (1937).

R. Payne, *The White Pony,* pp. 327-33, 354-8, 377-8.

*Alfred Hoffman, *Die Lieder des Li Yü 937-978, Herschers der sudlichen T'ang-Dynastie,* 274 pp. (1950).
_____, *Frühlingsblüten und Herbstmond,* 112 pp. (1951).

XV

DRAMA

The drama is a late development in Chinese literature. Though there are records of theatrical performances in the T'ang dynasty and earlier, the first complete drama texts date from the beginning of the Yüan (late thirteenth century). Yüan drama *(tsa-chü)* is a well-defined genre, the peculiarities of which may be traced to earlier forms. In Ming times (early fifteenth century) it was displaced in popularity by the Southern Drama *(nan-hsi,* or *hsi-wen)*, representing a separate tradition at least as old as the *tsa-chü*. After some four centuries of prominence it finally yielded to the Capital Theater *(ching-hsi)*, the type of play commonly seen in China today. These three types have certain basic features in common: they are all operatic productions in which sung and spoken parts alternate. They all include an orchestra and rely on elaborate costuming rather than stage sets. Popular plots and themes recur in all three.

In the development of these types the basic distinction is between Northern *(pei-ch'ü)* and Southern dramas *(nan-hsi)*. Primarily this division refers to regional types of music, but there are also structural differences. There was continual borrowing between competing forms so that by Ming times the fully developed Southern Drama showed strong northern influences, though essentially it had evolved from the southern *hsi-wen*. The three main types will be taken up in chronological order.

Pre-Yüan theatricals are known to have existed, but their nature is uncertain. No texts of the Chin dynasty *yüan-pen* have survived, and the Sung dynasty Variety Shows *(tsa-chü)* are known only from contemporary lists of the four acts of which they were regularly composed. The Yüan *tsa-chü* presumably borrowed the number of acts and the name, no longer appropriate for a play dependent on plotting rather than on displays of skill. The contribution of *yüan-pen* to the *tsa-chü* is even more a matter for speculation. It has been denied that there was any great similarity between the two, that the Chin *yüan-pen* represented a very rudimentary form. In the absence of any *yüan-pen* texts the question cannot be definitely decided, but the fact that contemporary sources list 280 titles of *yüan-pen* current in Chin times indicates their popularity. Furthermore early Yüan *tsa-chü* were also called *yüan-pen,* suggesting that the two were popularly associated.

Public entertainments in Sung times included narrative song recitations with percussion or string accompaniment. These recitations probably evolved from the T'ang *pien-wen,* originally popularized versions of Buddhist texts written in a mixture of prose and verse. The several forms of such recitations show a steady development from the Big Songs *(ta ch'ü),* a narrative sequence of *tz'u,* through the alternating *tz'u* and *shih* stanzas of the Turns *(chuan-t'a),* to the Drum Songs *(ku-tzu tz'u)* with both prose and *tz'u* songs. The best known of the Drum Songs is the *Shang-tiao tieh-lien-hua,* a version of the T'ang prose tale, *Hui chen chi,* built around ten stanzas of the *tz'u* "The Butterfly loves Flowers" *(tieh-lien-hua).* Each song is introduced by a prose narrative section paraphrased from the *Hui chen chi* and serves to express the sentiments of the characters in the situation described. The language of the *Tieh-lien-hua* is literary, and it is doubtful whether the work was recited to an unlettered audience. However, there is no doubt about the great popularity of the more elaborate Medley *(chu-kung-tiao),* developed from the Drum Song. Only one of the Medleys survives in complete form: the *Hsi-hsiang chu-kung-tiao* of the Chieh-yüan Tung, a man supposed to have lived during the Chin. Fragments of two others make possible a few generalizations about the form. Like the Drum Song, the Medley was a recitation of prose and verse with instrumental accompaniment. Its existence is attested as early as the beginning of the twelfth century, when professional specialists made their living from such recitations. The Medley was essentially a solo performance, the narrative being in the third person. The reciter had more in common with the story-teller than with the dramatic stage, but the *tsa-chü* has borrowed at least one feature from the Medley, the restriction of singing parts to the leading role.

Among the forerunners of the Yüan drama the Medley is the most significant literary form (leaving out of account the *yüan-pen).* Though not wholly in verse, it may be described as a narrative song-poem of epic length. The lyrical element of the plays comes directly from a shorter song form, successor to the *tz'u,* the *san-ch'ü. San-ch'ü* differs from *tz'u* in the nature of the tunes employed, in the use of a wider range of subject matter, and by the admission of a larger amount of colloquial language; the basic difference is that *san-ch'ü* does not observe the many rules which made *tz'u* a difficult form unsuitable for narration. Groups of tunes belonging to the same key were assembled into a "suite"

95

(*t'ao-shu*) to make a unit composition for which words could be supplied at will. Such musical units were incorporated into the Yüan drama, each act being constructed around one of them.

From these pre-existing materials the Yüan drama was created, though the *yüan-pen* may have been an intermediate stage. It is an operatic drama in four acts *(che)* with an optional fifth act *(hsieh-tzu)*, which may be placed before or after any of the other acts and which is free from the restrictions on singing parts observed in the other acts. Regardless of subject matter, the roles are limited to a few types, of which only the leading male or female role may sing, and only one of them in a given play. The action of the play relies on spoken dialog; the songs usually serve to express the feelings of the chief characters. The songs in any given act must belong to the same key and must be taken from a specific *t'ao-shu*. The musical pattern of the tunes is not as inflexible as that of the *tz'u*, and permits the insertion of spoken patter, consisting of clichés in colloquial language which serve to make the literary language of the songs more intelligible to the audience and which also aid in varying the rhythms.

There is evidence that the early Southern Drama (*hsi-wen*), originating in the Sung dynasty, continued to be produced in southern China throughout Yüan times, and toward the end of the Yüan even competed in the north with the *tsa-chü*. Songs from some 150 such southern plays have been preserved in anthologies and technical treatises, and three complete texts have survived in the *Yung-lo ta-tien*. These plays are of much looser construction than the Yüan *tsa-chü*, and diverge in the conventions observed. All characters are permitted to sing, and duets occur as well as solos. A brief prologue summarizes the plot. The songs do not form a *t'ao-shu*. None of the surviving texts is divided into acts, but from their greatly varying lengths it may be assumed that the number of acts was not fixed. The technical terms for roles are not the same as in *tsa-chü*.

All of these peculiarities are characteristic also of the developed Southern Drama of Ming times. However this drama (*k'un-ch'ü*) was a regularized version of the *hsi-wen*, with rules as definite as those governing the *tsa-chü*. The *k'un-ch'ü* was at first the least popular of four competing forms of Southern Drama, each characterized by a different regional type of music, until transformed by the efforts of a single man, Wei Liang-fu (early sixteenth century), a native of K'un-shan (near Suchow in Kiangsu) – whence the name. He was a musician who enlarged and standardized the orchestra, utilizing the tunes of his native district for operatic scores. Under his leadership the texts of *k'un-ch'ü* plays became more literary and elegant, and at the same time less "dramatic" than the *hsi-wen* or *tsa-chü*. *K'un-ch'ü* plays tended to be excessively long, often running to fifty or sixty "acts." Their success was ascribed by contemporary observers to the excellence of the music and its popularity with professional entertainers, a class commonly associated with the Suchow region. From the time of its origin in the second half of the sixteenth century until its decline in the nineteenth century it was the dominant dramatic form, attracting many writers of ability. Two schools of *k'un-ch'ü* are recognized, one stressing the music, the other relying on plot and poetic diction. Writers of the latter school produced the most famous plays: *The Peony Pavilion (Mu-tan t'ing)* by T'ang Hsien-tsu (1550-1617), *The Peach Blossom Fan (T'ao-hua shan)* by K'ung Shang-jen (1648-1708?), and *The Palace of Long Life (Ch'ang-sheng tien)* by Hung Sheng (1650?-1704).

By the eighteenth century *k'un-ch'ü* was declining in popularity, and several local forms began to attract the audiences. It was not until after the T'ai-p'ing rebellion (1848-1865) had devastated the Hangchow region, where actors were trained in the difficult *k'un-ch'ü* techniques and where most of the plays were written, that the *k'un-ch'ü* was entirely replaced by the Capital Theater *(ching-hsi)*. The latter, a composite of regional types of play is also known as *p'i-huang,* from the names of the several localities to which the music of the new plays was native. This music is loud and rather vulgar, compared with the refined airs of the *k'un-ch'ü.* The dialog of the Capital Theater is more colloquial, likewise the singing parts, though the latter retain a large element of literary language vocabulary. These plays are usually shorter and more dramatic than *k'un-ch'ü* plays, but are seldom presented in their entirety. A theater program is made up of a number of acts chosen from different plays for the purpose of giving a well-known actor a chance to appear in congenial roles.

Authorities

Ch'ien Chung-shu, "Tragedy in Old Chinese Drama," *T'ien Hsia Monthly (TH)* 1(1935).37-46.

Yao Hsin-nung, "Rise and fall of the K'un ch'ü," *TH* 2(1936).63-84.
——————, "The Theme and Structure of the Yüan Drama," *TH* 1(1935).388-403.

Wang Kuo-wei 王國維, *Sung Yüan hsi-ch'ü shih* 宋元戲曲史, 199 pp. (1915).

Wu Mei 吳梅, *Yüan chü yen-chiu ABC* 元曲研究, 125 pp. (1929).

*Aoki Masaru 青木正兒, *Shina kinsei gikyoku shi* 支那近世戲曲史, 904 pp. (1930).
——————, *Gennin zakugeki josetsu* 元人雜劇序説, 210 pp. (1937).

*Cheng Chen-to, "Lun pei-chü ti hsieh-tzu 論北劇的楔子," pp. 70-94 in *Chung-kuo wen-hsüeh lun chi* 中國文學論集 (1927).
——————, *Chung-kuo wen-hsüeh shih*, pp. 690-715, 832-932, 1122-46 (1932).
——————, *Chung-kuo su wen-hsüeh shih*, vol. 2, pp. 1-154 (1938).

*Yoshikawa Kōjirō 吉川幸次郎, *Gen zakugeki kenkyū* 元雜劇研究, 514 pp. (1948).

Translations

I. General

M. Bazin, *Théatre chinoise*, 409 pp. (1838) (Translation of four Yüan plays listed by title under II below).
——————, *Le siècle des Youên*, 574 pp. (1850) (Contains summaries of plays listed under II below).
Hans Rudelsberger, *Altchinesische Liebes-Komodien*, 116 pp. (1923) (Free adaptations of five Yüan plays listed below by title. All of the poems and songs are omitted, and the

dialog is frequently mutilated past recognition).

L. C. Arlington and Harold Acton, *Famous Chinese Plays*, 420
pp. (1937) (Translation of thirty-one modern *ching-hsi*
and two *k'un-ch'ü*).

II. *Tsa-chü*

A. Plays from the *Yüan ch'ü hsüan,* numbered in order of their
appearance there.

1. *Han kung ch'iu*
    J. F. Davis, *The Sorrows of Han,* 18 pp. (1829).

2. *Chin ch'ien chi*
    Bazin, *Siècle des Youên,* pp. 213-29 (Summary).

4. *Yüan-yang pei*
    Bazin, *Siècle,* pp. 230-7 (Summary).
    ? Rudelsberger, pp. 9-36.

5. *Chuan K'uai T'ung*
    Bazin, *Siècle,* pp. 237-9 (Summary).

6. *Yü ching t'ai*
    ? Rudelsberger, pp. 37-54.

8. *Ho han-shan*
    Bazin, *Théatre,* pp. 137-256.

9. *Hsieh t'ien hsiang*
    ? Rudelsberger, pp. 53-76.

18. *Lai sheng chai*
    Bazin, *Siècle,* pp. 249-61 (Summary).

19. *Hsieh jen kuei*
    Bazin, *Siècle,* pp. 261-8 (Summary).

22. *Lao sheng erh*
    Davis, *An Heir in his Old Age,* 115 pp. (1817).

29. *T'ieh-kuai Li*
    Bazin, *Siècle,* pp. 276-98 (Summary).
    ? Rudelsberger, pp. 77-96.

32. *Ch'iu hu hsi ch'i*

Bazin, *Siècle*, pp. 201-9 (Summary).

41. *Ch'ien nü li hun*
    Bazin, *Siècle*, pp. 215-320 (Summary).

45. *Huang liang meng*
    Bazin, *Siècle*, pp. 322-34 (Summary).
    ? Rudelsberger, pp. 97-111.

48. *Hao t'ien t'a*
    Bazin, *Siècle*, pp. 336-48 (Summary).

61. *Jen tzu chi*
    Bazin, *Siècle*, pp. 367-76 (Summary).

64. *Hui lan chi*
    Stanislas Julien, *Hoei-Lan-Ki, ou l'histoire du cercle de craie*, 149 pp. (1832).

66. *Tsou mei hsiang*
    Bazin, *Théatre*, pp. 3-134.

78. *Yü ju t'ao yüan*
    Bazin, *Siècle*, pp. 394-8 (Summary).

84. *Pao chuang ho*
    Bazin, *Siècle*, pp. 402-19 (Summary).

85. *Chao-shih ku-erh*
    S. Julien, *Tchao-Chi-Kou-Eul, ou l'orphelin de la Chine*, 131 pp. (1834).

86. *Tou o yüan*
    Bazin, *Théatre*, pp. 323-409.

94. *Huo lang tan*
    Bazin, *Théatre*, pp. 259-320.

B. *Hsi hsiang chi*

    S. I. Hsiung, *The Romance of the Western Chamber*, 218 pp. (1936).

III. *K'un-ch'ü*

    1. *Mu tan t'ing*
       Vincenz Hundhausen, *Die Rückkehr der Seele*, 3 vols.

187, 205, 252 pp. (1937).

2. *P'i-pa chi*

    M. Bazin, *Le Pi-Pa-Ki, ou l'histoire du luth,* 275 pp.
      (1841).

    V. Hundhausen, *Die Laute,* 469 pp. (1930).

3. Single scenes from *k'un-ch'ü* plays

    H. A. Acton, "*Ch'un-hsiang nao hsüeh,* Ch'un-hsiang
      turns the schoolroom topsy-turvey, a *k'un-ch'ü* light
      comedy from the Ming dynasty play Mu-tan t'ing," *TH*
      2.357-72.

    ——————, "Scenes from *Shih hou chi,*" *TH* 9.86-112.

    ——————, "Lin-ch'ung yeh-pen," *TH* 9.180-8.

    Arlington and Acton, *Famous Chinese Plays,* pp. 53-75,
      319-22.

XVI

POPULAR LANGUAGE FICTION: THE STORY AND THE NOVEL

Fiction in the literary language developed within the literary tradition and evolved a distinctive form, the *ch'uan-ch'i*. Popular language fiction was derived from the story-teller's tale, and at one point represented the transcription of an oral art with its own traditions and techniques into written form; later the story or story-cycle was expanded to make the long novel, which in turn provided the model for the artistic novel, a major literary form outside the main literary language tradition.

The earliest recorded examples of the story-teller's art date probably from the Sung dynasty, but it is likely that there had been story-tellers in China for as long as urban centers existed to support them. That their tales went unrecorded for centuries is not surprising. The story-teller addressed an essentially illiterate audience, as he does in China today. To put his stock-in-trade into writing was to lose his monopoly without increasing his income, since readers of tales written down as he recited them would chiefly be potential competitors; the professionally literate had no interest in a literature without standing or literary tradition, and for them the *ch'uan-ch'i* tale supplied the need for fiction in a socially tolerated form.

A precedent for attempting to write narrative in non-literary language, however, already existed. The professional story-teller was not the only one who addressed an illiterate audience. From the early period of the introduction of Buddhism into China, Buddhist missionaries and priests preached sermons in public, leaning heavily on Jataka tales and apologues to hold audiences incapable of following abstract expositions of doctrine. Scholarly priests devoted themselves to translating the Buddhist canon into literary Chinese; those engaged in proselytizing attempted to write their apologues in a language approximating the spoken. The resulting texts, known as "Popularizations" *(pien-wen)*, are of great importance as representing a transitional stage between the oral and the written colloquial language tale. Specimens dating from T'ang times have been recovered in the twentieth century among the mass of early manuscripts found in Tun-huang. Two types are represented, neither of any great intrinsic literary value. These are religious tracts—apologues based on sutras or saint's legends—and secular *pien-wen* obviously modeled after religious prototypes. Both are moral in tone, are liberally interspersed with doggerel verse, and are written in an awkward style lacking both the polish of the literary language and the flexibility of of the spoken. They could easily be the first attempts to write colloquial prose.

There is considerable contemporary evidence of the activities of story-tellers and popular entertainers in Sung times. The different lists and accounts are often obscure or contradictory in detail, but it is apparent that there was considerable special-ization in subject matter and that their performances enjoyed wide popularity. It was perhaps during the Sung period that an enter-prising publisher first saw an opportunity to exploit a new market by printing the prompt-books *(hua-pen)* used by the story-tellers; later appeared expanded versions of those prompt-books which were closer to the narrative as the story-tellers recited it, by analogy also called *hua-pen.* The earliest surviving *hua-pen* texts are to be sure considerably later, but conditions were favorable then for such a venture: by Southern Sung times printing had become sufficiently common to be used to reproduce more ephemeral books than the Classics and standard literary works. Times were prosperous, and at least in the flourishing commercial centers a large group of literate shopkeepers could be expected, men who were not sufficiently well educated to compete in the examinations, but who might want reading matter for entertainment within their ability to understand. In Yüan times, certainly, when the collo-quial language plays were being printed in large numbers, there was an established reading public for such literature.

Once published, the *hua-pen* became the model for story writers who were not professional story-tellers; like the *ch'uan-ch'i* the writing of *hua-pen* could be practiced by members of the scholar class as a pastime. Some were content to embellish existing *hua-pen;* others wrote new stories. Most of such stories as survive are contained in three late Ming collections collectively known as the *San-yen* (i.e., *Hsing-shih heng-yen, Ching-shih t'ung-yen, Yü-shih ming-yen*). A selection from these collections which remains popular, the *Chin-ku ch'i-kuan,* is the source for most Western language translations of colloquial language stories.

The *hua-pen* were probably the direct inspiration for the long historical and picaresque novels, *The Romance of the Three Kingdoms (San-kuo-chih yen-i)* and the *Shui hu chuan. Hua-pen* prototypes exist for both, but in their present form they represent a conscious reworking and expansion of the *hua-pen* versions at the hands of writers of considerable ability. The fact that there exist numerous variant editions of each makes any statement of traditional authorship of questionable value.

The *Romance of the Three Kingdoms* takes its plot from the historical conflict between the three successor states to the Han dynasty; the characters are all historical figures and the episodes elaborations of events recorded in the standard history of the period. The fictional version succeeds in bringing the actors to life and endowing their conflicts with real interest. It is written in a language that alternates between a simple literary language and dignified colloquial. Because of later additions it is impossible to give a date for the composition of this novel; the modern 120 chapter version is probably no earlier than late Ming times, but it may have existed in full-length novel form during the Yüan.

The *Shui hu chuan*, written in a purely colloquial language, deals with the exploits of a band of robbers during the early twelfth century. Some of the characters are historical, and the setting (Shantung) is geographically accurate.

The episodes related were derived from popular traditions. The novel shows inconsistencies in plotting and motivation that may be the result of trying to combine pre-existing and contradictory legends. It has been suggested that at least two story-cycles are involved, one centering about the activities of a robber band in Shantung, the other relating to another group in Shansi. The novel is not seriously weakened by these inconsistencies, as it depends for interest on picaresque incident rather than characterization; unity is imposed by a frame. The present edition in seventy chapters was edited in early Ch'ing times by Chin Sheng-t'an (?1610-1661) from one or more longer versions.

The *Record of a Journey to the West (Hsi yu chi)* also has antecedents in the story-teller's tale, but is the work of a known writer, Wu Ch'eng-en (*ca.* 1500-1580). Instead of treating realistically the adventures of popular heroes it presents allegorically the exploits of supernatural agents. The basis for the plot is the seventh century pilgrimage of the Buddhist priest Hsüan-tsang to India to obtain sacred texts. Hsüan-tsang's own record of his journey is an important firsthand description of central Asia and India in his day; his biography by a contemporary provides an inspiring description of a brave and devout man prepared to face any danger to accomplish his mission. The novel introduces Hsüan-tsang as such a character, and then confronts him with obstacles beyond the power of any mortal man to surmount. But if his opponents have become supernatural, his guides and assistants are also superhuman. A fabulous stone monkey, invulnerable and endowed with infinite resourcefulness, is the chief agent whereby Hsüan-tsang reaches his goal—not simply a far off country, but the Western Paradise—and Monkey is the real protagonist, leaving Hsüan-tsang a minor role, necessary to the plot but of secondary interest in its development. The style is naive, appropriate to a fairy tale, but the *Journey to the West* is not primarily a story for children. The allegorical pilgrimage is reminiscent of Bunyan, but there is in addition a strong undercurrent of satire which makes the *Journey to the West* an acute criticism of society and bureaucracy in the *ch'uan-ch'i* tradition.

The first novel of everyday life and also the first novel divorced from popular legend and historical event is the *Chin p'ing mei,* written in Ming times by an unknown author. To be sure it takes as a point of departure an episode from the *Shui hu chuan,* but the life it describes is that of a well-to-do business man bent on pleasure, whose deeds of heroism are limited to the bed-chamber. The *Chin p'ing mei* is known as a pornographic novel, and it contains passages which could not be characterized as anything but pornography. However, such passages make up a very small part of the 100 chapters of the whole novel, and they are functional within the profoundly moral purpose of the author. It is not pornography in that the pornographic element is not the excuse for the book—though it helps explain the book's popularity. Read in its entirety, the *Chin p'ing mei* appears as a terrifying exposure of the vanity of pleasure; by depicting the pleasures of the flesh in their most attractive form the author has made his grewsome denouement the more effective. The *Chin p'ing mei* is the first Chinese novel with convincing women characters. The treatment is not especially subtle, but the many women who figure in the novel are distinctly individual and consistent. The novel is written in a wooden and impersonal style appropriate to a naturalism that observes no reticences.

The *Dream of the Red Chamber (Hung lou meng)* is a romantic novel of 120 chapters begun by Ts'ao Chan (?-1763) and completed by Kao E (*ca.* 1795). It is in part autobiographical, the setting being derived from Ts'ao Chan's recollections of the prosperous

105

days of his youth. He died before he finished the novel, and the last forty chapters were supplied by Kao E on the basis of hints appearing in the first part. The semi-happy ending was probably not intended by Ts'ao Chan and considerably weakens the force of the novel. However, it is possible to read the book as a whole without being aware of its dual authorship, and it may properly be treated as a unit. The story follows the declining fortunes of a wealthy family of officials, providing an ominous setting of decaying luxury and extravagance for the love story which is the real plot. The hero is hardly more than a child during the seven years covered by the novel; he is sentimental, effeminate, and motivated chiefly by his need for affection. His two girl cousins supply the affection, but the favored one combines with it a jealousy and self-pity that finally destroy her. Much of the book is devoted to their quarrels, with an insight into the psychology of love that makes the *Dream of the Red Chamber* unique in Chinese literature. A multitude of sub-plots supply incident and variety of character.

Satire occurs as an element in the *Hsi yu chi,* but the satirical novel proper appears first in the Ch'ing dynasty with the *Unofficial History of Officialdom (Ju-lin wai-shih)* by Wu Ching-tzu (1701-1754). The *Unofficial History* is an attack on inefficiency and corruption among officials and on the hypocrisy which the author assumed to be essential to a successful career. The book is amorphous and plotless, consisting of a series of tenuously connected episodes enacted by a constantly changing cast of characters, all modeled after contemporaries of the author. Its only unity derives from its preoccupation with a single social group. The satire is effective, the more so in not departing too far from the possible. The weakness of the book is apparent when the author abandons satire and attempts to portray his ideal of upright behavior in the simple unambitious men with abominable manners and insufferable pride who appear in the prologue and epilogue.

The *Unofficial History of Officialdom* was the model for an even more vicious attack on the bureaucracy, the *Record of Manifestations in the Official World (Kuan-ch'ang hsien-hsing chi)* by Li Pao-chia (1867-1906), a journalist who died before completing his novel. In the sixty chapters that were finished there is portrayed not one honest official. Granting that corruption was widespread toward the end of the Ch'ing dynasty, it seems unlikely that it was as universal as the *Record of Manifestations*

implies. Like its predecessor, this work is made up of a series
of almost unconnected incidents, but the pervading tone of ruthless satire lends it a unity of mood that compensates for the
absence of plot. In a way the *Record of Manifestations* is an
obituary of the Ch'ing dynasty; no state could long survive a
fraction of the maladministration described in its pages.

Satire also occupies a prominent place in the *Travels of Lao-
ts'an (Lao-ts'an yu-chi)* by Liu E (1857-1909), a semi-autobi-
ographical novel by one of the most original and energetic of the
reformers of late Ch'ing times. The *Travels of Lao-ts'an* is a
reflection of Liu E's multiform interests, ranging from flood
control (treated allegorically) through music, philosophy, and
good government to crime detection and herbal medicine. Arthur
Conan Doyle was the inspiration for the murder-mystery episode,
and Liu E's novel provides the transitional link between the
traditional Chinese novel, evolved from the story-teller's tale,
and the modern Chinese novel, grafted onto imported foreign models
representing another line of development.

Authorities

I. General

Ou Itai, *Essai critique et bibliographique sur le roman chinois*, thèse pour le Doctorat de l'Université, 189 pp. (1933) (Based on Lu Hsün, *Chung-kuo hsiao-shuo shih-lüeh*).

T'an Cheng-pi, *Chung-kuo hsiao-shuo fa-ta shih*, 471 pp. (1934).

Kuo Chen-i, *Chung-kuo hsiao-shuo shih*, 2 vols., 712 pp. (1939).

II. *Pien-wen*

Jan Jaworski, "Notes sur l'ancienne littérature populaire en Chine," *Rocznik Orjentalistyczny* 12(1936).181-93.

Cheng Chen-to, *Chung-kuo su wen-hsüeh shih*, vol. 1, pp. 180-270.

III. *Hua-pen*

Jaroslav Prušek, "Popular Novels in the Collection of Ch'ien Tseng," *Archiv Orientální*, 10(1938).281-94.

——————, "The Narrators of Buddhist Scriptures and Religious Tales in the Sung Period," *ibid.*, 375-89.

——————, "Researches into the Beginnings of the Chinese Popular Novel," *ibid.*, 11(1939).91-132.

T'an Cheng-pi, *op. cit.*, pp. 207-83.

Iriya Yoshitaka 入矢義高 , "Wahon no seikaku ni tsuite" 話本の性格について , *Tōhō gakuhō* (Kyōto) 12 (1941).411-36.

IV. *San-yen* and *Chin-ku ch'i-kuan*

Paul Pelliot, "Le Kin Kou K'i Kouan," *T'oung Pao* 24(1925). 54-60.

Arthur Waley, "Notes on the History of Chinese Popular Literature," *TP* 28(1932).246-54.

V. Studies of specific novels

(No attempt has been made to list here the voluminous Japanese and Chinese language literature, but attention should be called to the excellent critical studies of texts and authorship of *Shui hu chuan*, *Hung lou meng*, *Hsi yu chi*, *San-kuo-chih yen-i*, *San-hsia wu-i*, *Kuan-ch'ang hsien-hsing chi*, *Erh-nü ying-hsiung chuan*, *Hai-shang-hua lieh-chuan*, and *Ching hua yuan* by Hu Shih 胡適 , collected in his *Wen ts'un*

文存 and separately published as *Chung-kuo chang-hui hsiao-shuo k'ao-cheng* 中國章回小説考證).

Hung lou meng

> Lee Chen Tong, *Étude sur le songe du pavillon rouge*, thèse pour le Doctorat de l'Université, 143 pp. (1934).
>
> · Kou Lin-Ke, *Essai sur le Hong Leou Mong (Le rêve dans le pavillon rouge)*, thèse...pour le Doctorat de l'Université, 174 pp. (1935).
>
> Lu Yueh Hwa, *La jeune fille chinoise d'après Hong-Leou-Mong*, thèse pour le Doctorat de l'Université, 107 pp. (1936).

Shui hu chuan

> Chao Ching-shen, "Some Recent Studies in *Shui hu chuan* or *The Story of the Water Margin*," *Philobiblion* 2.3(1948). 3-7.

Ju-lin wai-shih

> Ho Shih-chun, *Jou Lin Wai che, Le roman des lettrès, Étude sur un roman satirique chinois*, thèse pour le Doctorat d'Université, 195 pp. (1933).

Lao-ts'an yu-chi

> Harold E. Shadick, "The Travels of Lao Ts'an: A Social Novel," *Yenching Journal of Social Studies*, 2.1(1939). 39-69.
>
> C. S. Ch'ien, "A Note on the second chapter of Mr. Decadent," *Philobiblion* 2.3(1948).8-14.

Translations

I. *Hua-pen*

> Chi-chen Wang, *Traditional Chinese Tales*, pp. 115-42 *(Ts'o chan Ts'ui-ning, Nien-yü kuan-yin)*.

II. *San-yen*

> Harold Acton and Lee Yi-hsieh, *Four Cautionary Tales*, 159 pp. (1947).
>
> Chi-chen Wang, *Traditional Chinese Tales*, pp. 143-214.
>
> George Soulié de Morant, *Chinese Love Tales*, 163 pp. (1931).

III. *Chin-ku ch'i-kuan* (for a tabular listing of the many scattered translations from *Chin-ku ch'i-kuan,* cf. *Bibliotheca Sinica* 3.1763-1770).

> E. Butts Howell, *The Inconstancy of Madame Chuang,* 259 pp. (1925) (Nos. 3, 6, 19, 20, 27 from *Chin-ku ch'i-kuan*).
> ——————————, *The Restitution of the Bride,* 247 pp. (1926) (Nos. 4, 5, 9, 12, 22, 36 from *Chin-ku ch'i-kuan*).

IV. Major Novels

San-kuo-chih yen-i

> C. H. Brewitt-Taylor, *San Kuo* or *Romance of the Three Kingdoms,* 2 vols, 638, 623 pp. (1925).

Shui hu chuan

> Pearl Buck: *All Men are Brothers,* 1279 pp. (1937) (Complete translation of the eighty chapter version, but lacking the epilogue).
> J. H. Jackson, *Water Margin,* 2 vols., 917 pp. (1937) (Somewhat abridged).
> F. Kuhn: *Die Rauber von Liang schan Moor,* 834 pp. (Free translation and abridgment of the 100 chapter version).

Hsi-yu-chi by Wu Ch'eng-ên (*ca.* 1550)

> *Arthur Waley, *Monkey,* 306 pp. (1943) (Translation of chapters 1-12, 13-5, 18-9, 22, 37-9, 44-6, 47-9, 98-100).
> Timothy Richards, *A Mission to Heaven,* 362 pp. (1913) (Translation of chapters 1-7, summary of 8-100).

Feng-shen yen-i

> Wilhelm Grube, *Feng-shên-yên-i. Die Metamorphosen der Götter,* 2 vols., 657 pp. (1912) (Translation of chapters 1-46, summary of 47-100 by Herbert Mueller).

Chin p'ing mei

> Clement Egerton, *The Golden Lotus,* 4 vols., 387, 376, 385, 375 pp. (1939) (A complete translation, some passages in Latin).

Hung lou meng by Ts'ao Chan and Kao E

> *F. Kuhn, *Der Traum der roten Kammer,* 788 pp. (Considerably abridged, this remains the most complete translation to

date).

Chi-chen Wang, *Dream of the Red Chamber,* 371 pp. (1912)
(Translation of chapter one; the rest briefly summarized.
The introduction is useful).

H. Bancraft Joly, *Hung Lou Meng* or, *The Dream of the Red
Chamber, a Chinese Novel,* 2 vols., 378, 538 pp. (1892,
1893) (Expurgated but otherwise painfully literal translation of chapters 1-56).

Pao Wen-wei, "Le Rêve de la Chambre Rouge," *Études françaises*
4(1943).67-80, 149-61, 224-37, 306-17 (Translation of
chapter fifty-seven, with Chinese text).

Ching hua yuan by Li Ju-chen (*ca.* 1800)

Chi-chen Wang, "A voyage to Strange Lands," pp. 162-88 in
Chinese Wit and Humor (Excerpts).

Ju-lin wai-shih by Wu Ching-tzu (1701-1754)

Chi-chen Wang, "Two Scholars who Passed the Examinations,"
pp. 189-208 in *ibid.* (Chapter one of *Ju-lin wai-shih*).

Hsu Chen-ping, "Four Eccentrics: the Epilogue to *Ju Lin Wai
Shih,*" *T'ien Hsia Monthly* 11.2(1940).178-92.

Lao-ts'an yu-chi by Liu E (1857-1909)

H. Y. Yang and G. M. Tayler, *Mr. Derelict,* 167 pp. (1948)
(This translation omits chapters 9, 10, 11, 18, 19, and
part of 20).

Lin Yi-chin and Ko Te-shun, *Tramp Doctor's Travelogue,* 263
pp. (1939) (Somewhat abridged translation of the twenty
chapter version).

Lin Yutang, *A Nun of T'aishan, and other Translations,* pp.
1-112 (Contains a translation of six further chapters of the Lao-ts'an story published under the title
Lao-ts'an yu-chi erh-chi).

V. Unimportant novels available in translation

Hao ch'iu chuan

John Francis Davis, *The Fortunate Union,* 2 vols., 258, 211
pp. (1829).

F. Kuhn, *Eisherz und Edeljaspis, oder die Geschichte einer
glucklichen Gattenwahl,* 343 pp. (1926).

Yü chiao li

Stanislas Julien, *Les Deux Cousines*, 2 vols., 362, 335 pp. (1842).

P'ing shan leng yen

Stanislas Julien, *P'ing-chan-ling-yen—Les deux jeunes filles lettrées*, 2 vols., 360, 300 pp. (1860).

Erh tu mei

A. Théophile Piry, *Erh-tou-mei* ou *les pruniers merveilleux*, 2 vols., 334, 335 pp. (1880).

F. Kuhn, *Erh Tu Mei, oder die Wunder der zweiten Pflaumenbluten.*

Pai-she ching-chi

Stanislas Julien, *Pé-ché-Tsing-Ki, Blanche et Bleu, ou les deux couleuvres-fées*, 326 pp. (1834).

Yü ch'ing-t'ing

F. Kuhn, *Die Jadelibelle*, 294 pp. (1936).

THE LITERARY REVOLUTION

Modern Chinese literature is properly a separate field of study. It follows neither of the two traditions developed in China's past literature, the chief forms of which have been described in these pages. The treatment of modern Chinese literature here is limited to an account in general terms of the forces which shaped it and the major trends which it shows. For information about individual writers and existing translations of their works the reader is referred to the appended bibliography.

The significance of the Literary Revolution is best understood in terms of the literary traditions it has supplanted. From very early times most Chinese literature was written in a language which, because of its conciseness and grammatical structure, was intelligible only to the eye. During a period of at least two thousand years this literary language became more and more separated from the continually evolving spoken dialects, though its vocabulary was frequently enriched by borrowings from them. Forms and traditions were acknowledged as literature only as they were embodied in writings in the literary language. However, from Sung times on a popular language literature grew up, developing new forms—notably the novel and the drama—without counterparts in the literary language tradition and consequently not admitted as a part of literature. The language of these writings approximated actual speech, and so was intelligible to any reader who knew the requisite number of characters, though he might lack the knowledge of literary language grammar and the broad education necessary to read even the simplest texts in literary Chinese, heavily burdened with its long cultural tradition. The popular language literature, written for—but not often by—the barely literate, was from the first unencumbered with erudition; its exclusion from the literary canon left it free to develop along its own lines. By the twentieth century there existed a considerable body of writings in the popular language, without standing as literature, but with several highly evolved forms to its credit.

In the twentieth century when Chinese intellectuals began to read Western literatures, first in translation, and then in the original languages, they were struck by the prominent part occupied in them by forms which in China were not recognized as literature at all. While this contact with Western culture brought new insight into their own literature, the revaluation of traditional Chinese literature was only a by-product of what became a highly self-conscious reform movement, comparable in many ways with the *ku-wen* movement sponsored in the eighth century by Han Yü. In the early period, between the appearance in 1917 of the first polemics by Hu Shih and Ch'en Tu-hsiu urging the general use of written colloquial *(pai-hua)* and the Ministry of Education's decree of 1920 ordering that *pai-hua* be taught in the elementary schools, there was a bitter conflict between the reformers and the supporters of the literary language. The strength of the literary tradition was considerably weakened by the political chaos in which China found herself at the time, and the reformers could argue with justice that language reform was a part of the necessary modernization of China. From the beginning their program was based on social and political ideas derived from observation of Western institutions, ideas which gave the movement greater scope and significance than the purely literary or aesthetic issues involved. The surprisingly rapid success of the *pai-hua* movement was due in part to the zeal and brilliance of its advocates—mostly foreign educated—but chiefly to the desperate need for a written Chinese that would not absorb all of a student's time to master, so that students could be trained in the techniques and disciplines demanded by a new world. The abolition of the civil service examinations in 1908 had removed the channel through which a classical education could be turned into a successful career, so that in 1920 there was little reason other than habit for objecting to a more easily acquired literacy.

The virtual abandonment of literary Chinese as a medium for instruction and the use of *pai-hua* in text books was a great achievement; it remained to create a new *pai-hua* literature. Although there existed a native popular language literature with its own traditions, the writers of fiction, poetry, and drama during the twenties derived their models and inspiration from Western literature. One reason was the stimulus of new forms and ideas; another, the prestige enjoyed by Western studies generally. Further, it was not enough for a few reformers to insist that the Chinese novel was a respectable art form; a generation of polemics and propaganda was necessary before the dictum could go unquestioned. Meanwhile no such doubt attached to the corresponding Western forms, and there was every incentive to turn to them rather than to try to follow a Chinese tradition as yet without standing. The result of this wholesale borrowing was a literature at once derivative and immature. Few Chinese writers had a thorough knowledge of the Western literatures they were imitating; many relied on translations at second or third hand (usually through the Japanese), especially of the Russian authors, who exerted the most influence.

With all these handicaps, the new literature was still not free to develop and make its adjustments to an already complex literary environment. The same forces which had brought about language reform were operating on Chinese society as a whole, and the resulting disintegration of accepted standards and values, along with civil war and foreign encroachments, combined to convince Chinese artists and intellectuals that their efforts should all be directed toward achieving national stability, unity, and strength; that aesthetic values were of secondary importance. Consequently modern Chinese literature is predominantly doctrinaire; it is for the most part a weapon in the fight for social and political change, and tends to be strongly nationalistic, even when most derivative.

No single formula for national salvation has been universally accepted in China, and the conflicting creeds have all had their literary representatives. There has been a marked tendency for Chinese writers to form societies and cliques, each publishing a manifesto of principles and controlling one or more magazines as an outlet for the writings of the group. The detailed history of modern Chinese literature is best organized around these societies, which include practically all of the writers of note. The bewildering reversals of policy, the schisms and cliques that appear within originally harmonious groups, are a reflection of the complexity of the contemporary scene and the rapidity of change in China's intellectual life. However, one dominant trend has been apparent from the beginning of the literary revolution. More and more Chinese writers have turned to the left for their inspiration, abandoning both the anarchic aestheticism of the early Creation Society and the detached rationalism of the Crescent Moon Society. Some writers, including the greatest of them all, Lu Hsün, were forced into the revolutionary camp by the pressure of circumstance rather than out of intellectual conviction; others have openly advocated revolution from the beginning. But the dominant note of social protest occurs in every major writer of the new literature.

The achievement of the modern *pai-hua* movement can be assessed

115

only in terms of the milieu which produced it. It is easy to object that it has produced no major novel, that its poetry is diffuse, formless, and derivative, that only the short story has been practiced with a measure of success, and that only in the drama is there any sign of the creation of new forms or any attempt at utilizing materials from the native tradition. It is true that the acknowledged master of *pai-hua* literature, Lu Hsün, produced regrettably little in the way of creative writing, dissipating most of his energies in translation and polemic essays. On the other side there is the imposing bulk of writing published in China since 1920, produced despite conditions of war, political censorship, and economic insecurity hardly conducive to creative writing. There is the unmistakable advance in technique between the crude beginnings and work done in the thirties. And if there is no modern Chinese writer of sufficient stature to rank with the greatest ones of the past or with the half-dozen major contemporary Western writers, at least there are living today many Chinese who write with a high degree of competence, some with an impressive corpus of works to their credit, some who show promise of becoming important writers in the future.

The literary revolution as a movement is over; *pai-hua* is established beyond question as a vehicle for literature. There are signs that the period of direct imitation of foreign models is passing. While there is still room for experimentation, the movement has layed the foundation for a new literary tradition which will to a large extent determine the direction of Chinese literature as yet unwritten.

Authorities

I. General Studies

1. Nym Wales, "The Modern Literary Movement," Appendix A in *Living China,* pp. 335-55.

2. "Main currents in Chinese literature, 1917-37," *China Institute Bulletin* 5.1(Oct., 1940).9-10 (Review of a work in Chinese by Li Ho-lin).

3. "Recent literature in China," *ibid.,* 5.2(Nov., 1940).12-5 (A survey of early wartime writers).

4. Hsiao Chi'en, *Etching of a Tormented Age—A Glimpse of Contemporary Chinese Literature,* 48 pp. (1942) (A eulogistic propaganda piece).

5. D. L. Phelps, "Letters and Arts in the War Years," chapter 27 in *China,* (edited by H. F. MacNair) pp. 406-19 (1946).

6. Joseph Schyns, ed., *Romans à lire et romans à proscrire,* 297 pp. (1946) (The Introduction pp. 20-37 contains a survey of modern writing. The bulk of the work is devoted to brief synopses of Chinese novels and collections of stories and plays. *Cf.* review in *HJAS* 9(1947).378-9).

*7. J. Schyns, ed., *150C Modern Chinese Novels and Plays,* lviii, 484 pp. (1948) (A translation into English of (6), greatly augmented. Pp. i-lviii: Su Hsueh-lin, "Present day fiction and drama in China." Pp. 1-116: Chao Yen-sheng, "Short biographies of authors." Index in Chinese to titles).

*8. Henri van Boven, *Histoire de la littérature chinoise moderne,* 187 pp. (1946) (The most complete Western language survey. Based largely on secondary sources, it is not always reliable but is indispensable as a guide).

9. O. Brière, S. J., "Les tendences dominantes de la littérature chinoise contemporaine," *Bulletin de l'Université l'Aurore* 3.9(July, 1948).234-69 (Concerned primarily with ideology).

10. Lao She, "The Modern Chinese Novel," *National Reconstruction,* 7.1(July, 1946).

11. Chen Ta-jen, "Literature chronicle," *T'ien Hsia Monthly* 6(1938).228-30 (Brief notes).

12. "A travers le monde des livres chinois (1940-1949)," *Bulletin de l'Université l'Aurore* 3.10(1949).87-103 (The section on literature contains notes on recently published fiction and plays).

II. Studies of Individual Writers (Refer also to the entries under I)

A. Lu Hsün

*1. Chi-chen Wang, "Lusin, A Chronological Record 1881-1936," *China Institute Bulletin* 3.4(1939).99-125 (An abridgment of this, the best study and appreciation of Lu Hsün in English, appears as the introduction to *Ah Q and Others*).

2. O. Brière, "Un écrivain populaire: Lou Sin," *Bulletin de l'Université Aurore* 3.7(1946).51-78.

3. Edgar Snow, "Lu Hsün," pp. 21-8 in *Living China*, reprinted from *Asia*, Jan. 1935.

4. "In Memory of Lu Hsün," "The Correspondence of Lu Hsün," *China Institute Bulletin* 2.3(1937).85-8 (Reviews of two Chinese language publications).

5. Yao Hsin-nung, "Lu Hsün, his life and works," *TH* 3(1936). 348-57.

B. Mao Tun

1. O. Brière, "Un peintre de son temps: Mao T'oen," *Bulletin de l'Université l'Aurore* 3.4(1943).236-56.

C. Pa Chin

1. O. Brière, "Un romancier chinois contemporain: Pa Kin," *ibid.*, 3.3(1942).577-98.

D. Su Mei

1. O. Brière, "Sou Mei ou Lou I: ses contes et sa critique," *ibid.*, 3.4(1943).920-33.

E. Lao Shê

1. George Kao, "The Novels of Lao Sheh," *China Institute Bulletin* 3.7-8(1939).184-9 (A brief biographical note

with summaries and criticism of three early novels).

F. Ting Ling

    1. Earl H. Leaf, "Ting Ling, Herald of a New China," *TH* 5(1937).225-36.

III. Drama

  A. General (*cf.* also entries 5, 7, and 8 under I)

    1. Yao Hsin-nung, "Drama Chronicle," *TH* 3(1936).45-52.

    2. Frank B. Wells, "Drama Chronicle," *ibid.*, 6(1938).475-9.

    3. Liang Yen, "Drama Chronicle," *ibid.*, 7(1938).177-80 (War-time activities).

    4. Ling Ai-mei, "Drama Chronicle," *ibid.*, 10(1940).256-9.

    5. "Synopses of four recent plays," *China Institute Bulletin* 5.3(Dec., 1940).22-30.

  B. Individual dramatists

    1. Ts'ao Yü

      a. Gérard de Boll, "L'universe de Ts'ao Yu," *Collectanea de la Commission Synodale,* 17.1(Jan., 1944).175-88.

IV. Poetry

    1. Harold Acton and Ch'en Shih-hsiang, *Modern Chinese Poetry,* Duckworth, London, 1936, 176 pp. (Contains an introduction and biographical notes on authors translated).

    2. Zau Sinmay, "Poetry Chronicle," *TH* 3(1936).263-9; 5(1937). 400-3.

    3. Ling Tai, "Poetry Chronicle," *TH* 7(1938).492-5.

    4. Robert Payne, *Contemporary Chinese Poetry,* Routledge, London 1947, 168 pp.

Translations

I. Anthologies of Stories

    1. J. B. Kin Yn Yu, *Anthologie des conteurs chinois modernes,* Rieder, Paris, 1929 ("Les Prosateurs Etrangers

Modernes") 190 pp. (Adaptations and free translations of nine authors. Translated into English as *The Tragedy of Ah Qui*, 1931).

2. Edgar Snow, *Living China, Modern Chinese Short Stories*, John Day, New York, 1936, 21-333 pp. (Free translations of fifteen representative authors, with biographical notes).

3. Chi-chen Wang, *Contemporary Chinese Stories*, Columbia University Press, New York, 1944, 227 pp. (Biographical and critical notes on the eleven authors translated, pp. 237-42).

4. Chun-chan Yeh, *Three Seasons and other Stories*, Staples Press, London, 1946 (Translations of five modern writers).

5. Yuan Chia-hua and Robert Payne, *Contemporary Chinese Short Stories*, Transatlantic Arts, London, 1946, 170 pp. (Stories by nine writers).

6. Chi-chen Wang, *Stories of China at War*, Columbia University Press, New York, 1947, 158 pp. (Thirteen authors translated by various hands).

7. George Kao, ed., *Chinese Wit and Humor*, Coward McCann, New York, 1946 (Pp. 275-384 contain translations of modern stories).

II. Translations of Stories and Novels (*cf.* V for full titles of anthologies)

Chang T'ien-i (1907-   )

Mutation
   Living China, pp. 267-89.
The Breasts of a Girl
   Yuan and Payne, pp. 97-117.
The Road
   Wang, pp. 1-8.
The Inside Story
   ibid., pp. 9-17.
Smile
   ibid., pp. 108-18.
Reunion
   ibid., pp. 119-26.

A New Life
    Stories of China, pp. 133-44.

Ch'en Shou-chu

    Three Men
        ibid., pp. 13-26.

Ching Yu-ling

    In the Steel Mill
        ibid., pp. 87-91.

Fei Ming (Feng Wen-ping) (1901-   )

    Little Sister
        Wang, pp. 127-34.

Hsiao Ch'ien

    The Conversion
        Living China, pp. 228-46.

Hsiao Hung

    Hands
        Richard L. Jen, *TH* 4(1937).498-514.

Hsieh Wen-ping

    The Patriot
        R. L. Jen, *TH* 3(1936).168-86.

Kuo Mo-jo (1891-   )

    Dilemma
        Living China, pp. 290-300.
    Under the Moonlight
        Stories of China, pp. 152-8.

Lao Hsiang (Wang Hsiang-ch'en)

    National Salvation through Haircut
        Chinese Wit and Humor, pp. 336-9.
    A Country Boy Withdraws from School
        Wang, pp. 18-24.
    Salt, Sweat and Tears
        Lin Yutang, *A Nun of Taishan and other Translations,*
        pp. 135-40.

Lao She (Shu Ch'ing-ch'un) (1898-   )

Rickshaw Boy, Reynal and Hitchcock, New York, 1945, 315 pp. (Translation by Evan King of *Lo-t'o hsiang-tzu*).

Black Li and White Li
 Wang, pp. 25-39.
The Glasses
 ibid., pp. 40-6.
The Philanthropist
 ibid., pp. 60-6.
Liu's Court
 ibid., pp. 67-79.
They Take Heart again
 Stories of China, pp. 96-106.
Portrait of a Traitor
 ibid., pp. 107-26.
The Letter from Home
 ibid., pp. 126-32.
Dr. Mao
 Chinese Wit and Humor, pp. 309-27.
Talking Pictures
 ibid., pp. 305-9.

Li Wei-t'ao

Test of Good Citizenship
 Stories of China, pp. 92-5.

Ling Shu-hua

The Helpmate
 Wang, pp. 135-42.
What's the Point of it?
 The author and Julian Bell, *TH* 3(1936).53-62.
A Poet goes Mad
 The author and J. Bell, *TH* 4(1937).401-21.
Writing a Letter
 Tr. by the author, *TH* 5(1937).508-13.

Lo Hua-sheng (Hsü Ti-shan) (1893-1941)

Après le crépuscule
 Kin, pp. 31-46.

Lu Hsün (Chou Shu-jen) (1881-1936)

Ah Q and Others, Columbia University Press, New York, 1941, 219 pp. (Translation by Chi-chen Wang of eleven stories, listed separately below).

Ah Q
George Kin Leung, *The True Story of Ah Q,* Commercial
Press, Shanghai, 1933, 90 pp.
Kin, pp. 79-124.
Ah Q and Others, pp. 77-129.

Looking Back to the Past
Feng Yu-sing, *TH* 6(1938).148-59.

Medicine
Living China, pp. 30-40.

A Little Incident
ibid., pp. 41-3.

K'ung I-chi
ibid., pp. 44-50.
Kin, pp. 67-76.

Divorce
Living China, pp. 85-96.
Ah Q and Others, pp. 31-44.

Benediction
ibid., pp. 51-4.
ibid., pp. 184-204.

Kites
Living China, pp. 75-7.

Mother's
ibid., pp. 78-84.

The Cake of Soap
Ah Q and Others, pp. 16-30.

Reunion in a Restaurant
ibid., pp. 45-58.

The Story of Hair
ibid., pp. 59-64.

Cloud over Luchen
ibid., pp. 65-76.

A Hermit at Large
ibid., pp. 130-57.

Remorse
ibid., pp. 158-83.

The Diary of a Madman
ibid., pp. 205-19.

The Dawn
C. C. Wang, *The Far Eastern Magazine,* March, 1940.

Warning to the Populace

C. C. Wang, *The China Journal*, June, 1940.
Professor Kao
    ibid., July, 1940.
A Happy Family
    ibid., August, 1940.

Lu Yen (Wang Heng)

Good Iron is not for Nails
    R. L. Jen, *TH* 10(1940).168-78.

Mao Tun (Shen Yen-ping) (1896-   )

Zwielicht in Schanghai (A translation of *Tzu-yeh* by
?F. Kuhn).

Suicide
    Living China, pp. 128-41.
Mud
    ibid., pp. 142-53.
Spring Silkworms
    Three Seasons, pp. 9-25.
    Wang, pp. 143-58.
Autumn Harvest
    Three Seasons, pp. 26-52.
Winter Fantasies
    ibid., pp. 53-72.
A True Chinese
    Wang, pp. 159-64.
Les Illusions
    Kin, pp. 155-76.
Heaven has Eyes
    China at War, pp. 27-38.

Pa Chin (Li Fei-kan) (1905-   )

Dog
    Living China, pp. 174-81.
The Puppet Dead
    Wang, pp. 80-94.
Star
    R. L. Jen, *TH* 5(1937).68-78, 193-267, 313-25, 464-
    514.

Pai P'ing-chieh

Builders of the Burma Road

Stories of China, pp. 76-86.

Ping Hsin (Hsieh Wan-ying) (1902-   )

    The First House Party
        R. L. Jen, *TH* 4(1937).294-306.
    Ennui
        Kin, pp. 145-52.

Ping Po

    An unsuccessful Fight
        Stories of China, pp. 47-53.

Sha Ting (Yang T'ung-fang) (1904-   )

    Voyage Beyond Law
        Living China, pp. 320-33.

Shen Ts'ung-wen (1903-   )

    The Chinese Earth; Stories by Shen Tseng-wen, translated by Ching Ti and Robert Payne, Allen and Unwin, London, 1947, 289 pp. (Fourteen stories, listed separately below).

    Pai tzu
        Living China, pp. 182-90.
        The Chinese Earth, pp. 15-21.
    The Lamp
        Yuan and Payne, pp. 67-86.
        The Chinese Earth, pp. 22-40.
    Under Cover of Darkness
        Yuan and Payne, pp. 87-96.
    Night March
        Wang, pp. 95-107.
    Hsiao-hsiao
        Lee Yi-hsieh, *TH* 7(1930).295-309.
    Old Mrs. Wang's Chickens
        Shih Ming, *TH* 10(1940).274-80.
        The Chinese Earth, pp. 61-9.
    Green Jade and Green Jade
        Emily Hahn and Shing Mo-lei, *TH* 2(1936).93-107, 174-96, 271-99, 360-90.
        The Chinese Earth, pp. 190-286.
    The Husband
        ibid., pp. 41-60.

San-San
ibid., pp. 70-87.
Under Moonlight
ibid., pp. 88-102.
The White Kid
ibid., pp. 103-13.
Three Men and a Girl
ibid., pp. 114-36.
Lung Chu
ibid., pp. 137-51.
The Lovers
ibid., pp. 152-9.
The Fourteenth Moon
ibid., pp. 160-6.
The Rainbow
ibid., pp. 177-89.

Shih Che-ts'un (1903-   )

The Waning Moon
Yuan and Payne, pp. 41-7.

Shih Ming

Fragment from a Lost Diary
Living China, pp. 302-18.

Sun Hsi-chen (1906-   )

Ah Ao
ibid., pp. 191-204.

T'ien Chün (Hsiao Chün) (1908-   )

Village in August, Smith and Durrell, New York, 1942,
313 pp. (Translation by ?Evan King of *Pa-yueh ti
hsiang-ts'un*).

Aboard the S.S. "Dairen Maru"
Living China, pp. 207-11.
The Third Gun
ibid., pp. 212-21.

T'ien Tao

Hou Fumakow
Lucien Mao, *TH* 11(1940).281-4.

Ting Ling (Chiang Ping-chih) (1902-   )

    The Flood
        Living China, pp. 154-64.
    News
        ibid., pp. 165-73.

Tuan-mu Hung-liang (Ts'ao Chih-lin)

    The Sorrow of the Lake of Egrets
        Yuan and Payne, pp. 118-29.
    Tiger
        ibid., pp. 130-46.
    Beyong the Willow Wall
        Stories of China, pp. 1-12.
    House Hunting
        ibid., pp. 145-51.

Wang Ssu-tien

    Liew shih
        Lucien Mao, *TH* 10(1940).260-4.

Wu Yen

    Departure
        Cicio Mar, *TH* 8(1939).260-6.

Yang Shuo

    Purge by Fire
        Stories of China, pp. 66-75.

Yao Hsüeh-yin (1909-   )

    The Half-baked
        Yuan and Payne, pp. 155-69.
    Half a Cartload of Straw Short
        Three Seasons, pp. 73-86.
    Chabancheh Makai
        Stories of China, pp. 54-65.

Yao Ying

    On My Library
        Lin Yutang, *op. cit.*, pp. 141-8.
    Summer in Nanking
        ibid., pp. 149-55.

Yang Chen-sheng (1890-   )

    The Anchor
       Yuan and Payne, pp. 26-40.
    Yuchun
       Wang, pp. 196-228.
    Revenge
       Ma P'ing-ho and Emily Hahn, *TH* 6(1938).480-91.

Yeh Shao-chün (1893-   )

    Mrs. Li's Hair
       Wang, pp. 165-73.
    Neighbors
       ibid., pp. 174-80.
    A Man Must Have a Son
       R. L. Jen, *TH* 6(1938).377-87.

Yü P'ing-po

    The Florist
       Mingtai Wu, *TH* 3(1936).63-7.

Yü Ta-fu (1896-   )

    Wistaria and Dodder
       Living China, pp. 247-66.
    Un désenchanté
       Kin, pp. 179-90.

III. Translations of Plays

1. Ts'ao Yü (Wan Chia-pao) (1905-   )

    a. *Thunder and Rain,* tr. by Yao Hsin-nung, *TH* 3(1936).270-95, 363-411, 486-530; 4(1937).61-95, 176-221.
    b. *The Sunrise,* a play in four acts tr. by H. Yonge, Commercial Press, Shanghai, 1940, 189 pp.

2. Yao Hsin-nung (Yao K'o)

    a. "When the Girls Come Back," tr. by the author, *TH* 7 (1938).94-120.

3. Hsiung Fo-hsi (1900-   )

    a. "Der Schlächter," tr. by W. Eichhorn, *Chinesisches Bauernleben,* Tokyo, 1938, pp. 3-53.
    b. "Ein Held vom Lande," *ibid.,* pp. 55-100.

c. "Das Rind," *ibid.*, pp. 101-61.

4. T'ien Han (1898-   )

"Der Kriegskamerad," tr. by Liao Bao-seing, *Sinica* 14(1939).165-92.

5. Ping Hsin

"Die erste Einladung," tr. by W. Eberhard, *Sinica* 10 (1935).266-74.

6. Lao She and Chao Ching-k'o

"Fruits in the Spring," tr. by George Kao, *China Magazine* 17.3(1947).37-53, 4.37-48, 5.37-50, 6.37-48.

ADDENDA AND CORRIGENDA

Page	Line	
5	26	*add* B. Karlgren, "The Book of Documents," *BMFEA* 22(1950). 1-81.
13	25	*for Fa yen,* etc. *read* Yang Hsiung's *Fa yen (Worte strenger Ermahnung),* (1939).
	29	*for Li Shao read Liu Shao.*
20	13	*add* R. P. Kramers, *K'ung Tzu Chia Yü,* 394 pp. (1950).
21	2	*add* A. R. O'Hara, *The Position of Woman in Early China according to the Lieh nü chuan,* 251 pp. (1945).
	5	*add* J. R. Hightower, *The Han shih wai chuan,* 350 pp. (1952).
29	1	*after* comparable *add* as poetry.
30	23	*for JNCBRAS* 54 *read JNCBRAS* 59.
32	33	*after* C. 4. *add* 5. The Exalted Man (Ta jen fu) von Zach, *Deutsche Wacht,* Dec., 1931.
35	28	*under* U. 2. *substitute* Achilles Fang, "Rhymeprose on Literature: the *Wen-fu* of Lu Chi," *HJAS* 14(1951). 527-66.
37	9	*under* III. *add* Po Chü-i (772-846) R. des Rotours, *Le traite des examens,* pp. 335-42 (1932).
48	21	*under* 2. *substitute* Achilles Fang, "Rhymeprose on Literature," *HJAS* 14(1951).527-66.
58	31	*under* 40. *add* William Acker, *T'ao the Hermit,* pp. 45-134 (1952).
68	11	*for* (1928) *read* (1919).
75	11	*for Genus read Gems.*
83	9	*add* 6. A. Waley, *The Real Tripitaka,* pp. 173-83 (1952).
109	14	*add* Richard Irwin, *The Evolution of a Chinese Novel: Shui-hu-chuan,* 223 pp. (1952).
	13, 24	*for Philobiblion read Philobiblon.*
110	14	*for* eighty *read* seventy.
	19	*for* 100 *read* 120.
114	26	*for* 1908 *read* 1905.
116	25	*for* layed *read* laid.
127	2	add *When I was in Sha Chuan and other Stories,* translated by Kung Pusheng, 110 pp. (1945).

Numbers in italics refer to translations, those in boldface to the page where the genre, book or author in question is discussed.

131

133

135

137

141